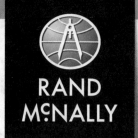

W9-BVN-540

2020

Road Atlas

Contents

Travel Information

National Parks ii-xiii
Our editors' picks of America's 60 national parks—big and small, west and east—showcase this country's astonishing beauty, highlight essential visitor information, and offer insightful travel tips.

Tourism Contacts xiv
Phone numbers and websites for tourism information in each state and province.

Road Construction and Road Conditions Resources xv
Numbers to call and websites to visit for road information in each state and province.

Hotel Resources 81

Mileage Chart 82
Driving distances between 77 North American cities.

Mileage and Driving Times Map inside back cover
Distances and driving times between over a hundred North American cities.

Maps

Map legend inside front cover

United States overview map 2-3

U.S. states 4-53

Canada overview map 54-55

Canadian provinces 56-63

Mexico overview map and Puerto Rico 64

U.S. and Canadian cities 65-80

Photo credits: p. ii (clockwise from top) ©Lijuan Guo Photography / Getty, ©Hage Photo / Getty, ©Image courtesy of Jeffrey D. Walters / Getty; p. iv (clockwise from top) ©Joshua Miller / Getty, ©www.sierralarn.com / Getty, ©Kyle Sparks / Getty; p. vi (clockwise from top) ©Matteo Colombo / Getty, ©Joe Rockey, ©Michael DeYoung / Getty; p. viii (clockwise from top) ©MargaretW / Getty, ©Photo Alto / Jerome Gorin / Getty, ©Jay Mayne / EyeEm / Getty; p. x (clockwise from top) ©Joecho_16 / Getty, ©nps, ©joe daniel price / Getty; p. xii (clockwise from top) ©zrfphoto / Getty, ©Nancy Nehring / Getty, ©zrfphoto / Getty; p. xiii ©zrfphoto / Getty; p. xiv (t to b) ©Gradyreese / Getty, ©Bluejayphoto / Getty; p. 81 (t to b) ©benedek / Getty, ©Zxvisual / Getty.

Published and printed in U.S.A.

For licensing information and copyright permissions, contact us at permissions@randmcnally.com

If you have a comment, suggestion, or even a compliment, please visit us at randmcnally.com/contact
or write to:
Rand McNally Consumer Affairs
P.O. Box 7600
Chicago, Illinois 60680-9915

1 2 3 BU 20 19

SUSTAINABLE FORESTRY INITIATIVE **Certified Sourcing**
www.sfiprogram.org
SFI-00993
This Label Applies to Text Stock Only

NATIONAL PARKS

America's 60 national parks not only inspire wonder and awe but also restore our souls. Here are 6 of our favorite parks—big and small, west and east—that showcase this country's astonishing beauty.

DENALI NATIONAL PARK & PRESERVE
ALASKA

This vast tract of central Alaskan outback surrounds North America's highest point: the park's 20,310-foot namesake peak, which translates to "the tall one" and "mountain-big" in Native Alaskan languages. No park in the lower 48 is as untouched: The only way to traverse its one road is via shuttle bus, which lets you truly focus on the sweeping tundra and mountain scenery.

1. Fall color of Denali and Wonder Lake. **2.** Brown bear near Mt. Galen. **3.** Hiker crossing Sunrise Creek in the Thorofare River valley.

GETTING ORIENTED

Denali is west of AK 3 (aka George Parks Highway). Gateway airports include Ted Stevens Anchorage International (243 miles south) and Fairbanks International (120 miles north). **Denali Visitor Center** is just inside the park's one entrance, on the east side. **Eielson Visitor Center** (Mile 66, Park Rd.) is 66 miles west of the entrance. **Walter Harper Talkeetna Ranger Station** (B St., Talkeetna, 907/733-2231) is 152 miles south of the park.

A few in-park wilderness lodges operate on inholdings (private lands), including **Camp Denali** (Mile 92, Park Rd., 907/683-2290, campdenali.com). Reservations (800/622-7275, www.reservedenali.com) are recommended at the park's six campgrounds. Nearby towns with amenities include **Healy** (www.denalichamber.com), 11 miles north of the park entrance, and **Talkeetna** (www.talkeetnachamber.org), 152 miles south. **Park Contact Info:** *907/683-9532, www.nps.gov/dena.*

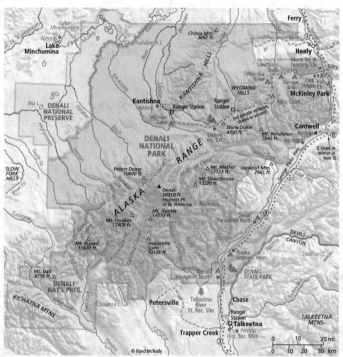

Atlas map **p. 5, C-3**

PARK HIGHLIGHTS

Natural Attractions. The minds behind Denali National Park made a bold decision when they chose to ban passenger cars from entry, and it has paid off in an authentic wilderness with an intact ecosystem. The prime visiting season runs from early June to mid-September.

It's hard to ignore **Denali** (formerly known as Mt. McKinley), the park's massive centerpiece. While other peaks are higher, the more than 18,000-foot ascent from Denali's surrounding lowlands is greater than Mt. Everest's rise above the Tibetan Plateau. The park's boundaries encompass numerous other peaks of the Alaska Range, including 17,400-foot **Mt. Foraker**, North America's sixth-highest peak, and the glaciated, 13,220-foot **Mt. Silverthrone** on the park's east side.

Treeless **tundra** atop perpetually frozen permafrost dominates the landscape. Below 3,000 feet, a 6-foot thicket of dense brush can cover the tundra; above 3,000 feet, alpine tundra has less vegetation and is easier to traverse on foot. Fed by glaciers and mountain snow, numerous **braided rivers**—including the Toklat, Savage, and Teklanika—are so named for their multiple, ever-changing channels in wide gravel floodplains that crisscross the tundra.

Denali is also a prime **wildlife habitat**. You may see grizzly bears and many hoofed mammals—such as moose, Dall sheep, and caribou—roaming the tundra.

Trails, Drives & Viewpoints. Denali is a hiker's paradise but has few developed trails; many routes follow the braided rivers. **Stony Creek** (Mile 60, Park Rd.) makes a great access point for exploring the tundra or mountains; the first 3 miles are relatively flat. Near the park entrance, the difficult 5-mile round trip to the **Mt. Healy Overlook** culminates in sweeping views of the Alaska Range.

Although Park Road is closed to private vehicles, the two-lane **Denali Highway** (aka AK 8) runs parallel to the Alaska Range for 135 miles from Paxson to Cantwell, 27 miles south of the park entrance. Only 22 miles of the highway are paved; the rest is gravel. The entire highway, however, stretches along jaw-dropping scenery and offers countless opportunities for wildlife watching, hiking, and boating. The main route to the park from either Anchorage or Fairbanks, the **George Parks Highway** also has plenty of spellbinding views.

Denali National Park & Preserve, AK

Programs & Activities. The park concessionaire operates **shuttle buses** (800/622-7275, www.reservedenali.com) that go as far as Kantishna (92 miles one-way, 13 hours round-trip) and offers some bus tours. Reserve shuttles and tours; two-thirds of the seats are sold in advance. Ranger-led **Discovery Hikes**, available daily in summer, are for experienced hikers only; sign up in person at the Denali Visitor Center.

Offering a different perspective, the **Alaska Railroad** (800/544-0552, www.alaskarailroad.com) runs between Anchorage and Fairbanks, stopping near the park entrance daily in summer. You can see Denali from above on a "flightseeing" trip with **Denali Air** (907/683-2261, denaliair.com) that departs from a private airstrip near the park entrance. **Denali Outdoor Center** (907/683-1925, www.denalioutdoorcenter.com) guides rafting trips on the Nenana River, just east of the park.

JOSHUA TREE NATIONAL PARK
CALIFORNIA

Trees that aren't trees. Boulders that look like skulls. A vast, dry plateau hiding an oasis. Distant snowcapped peaks. Welcome to weird, wild, wonderful Joshua Tree, named for the tall, Dr. Seuss–like trees that are actually flowering yucca plants. It's also home to cacti, piñon pines, cottonwoods, bighorn sheep, and many bird species. What's more, spectacularly starry night skies make this park a 24/7 masterpiece.

1. Joshua tree landscape. **2.** Climbing. **3.** Cholla cacti.

GETTING ORIENTED

The **Joshua Tree Visitor Center** is 142 miles east of Los Angeles International Airport and 39 miles northeast of smaller Palm Springs International Airport via I-10 and Twentynine Palms Highway (CA 62); 16 miles farther east along CA 62, near the town of **Twentynine Palms** (www.ci.twentynine-palms.ca.us), is the **Oasis of Mara Visitor Center**. The southern **Cottonwood Visitor Center** is 26 miles east of **Indio** (www.discoverindio.com) off I-10.

Make reservations for the popular **Black Rock** (99 sites) and **Indian Cove** (101 sites) campgrounds through Recreation.gov; other campgrounds are first-come, first-served. Lodgings abound in trendy **Palm Springs** (www.visitpalmsprings.com) and along CA 62 in **Yucca Valley** (www.yucca-valley.org), **Joshua Tree** (www.joshuatreechamber.org), and Twentynine Palms. **Park Contact Info:** *760/367-5500, www.nps.gov/jotr.*

PARK HIGHLIGHTS

Natural Attractions. Joshua Tree's striking scenery is due in no small part to the fact that it stretches between parts of two famous deserts: the higher-in-elevation Mojave to the north, and the lower-in-elevation Colorado to the south. Temperatures are high June through September, so try to visit October through May.

Joshua trees are everywhere but are especially striking in the park's northwestern section; bizarre boulder formations dot the northeastern section. The southern section, in and around Cottonwood Visitor Center, occasionally closes due to flash floods. Nevertheless, it's worth exploring some excellent trails through the cottonwoods. This is also a premier birding spot; more than 250 species have been recorded in the park.

Trails, Drives & Viewpoints. The 25-mile drive along scenic **Park Boulevard**, which connects the two northern park entrances and visitor centers, can be done in 40 minutes without stopping. Don't do that, since you'd miss, well, virtually everything, including the curvaceous **Arch Rock** (an easy 0.5-mile loop walk); the pockmarked mounds of **Skull Rock** (a moderate 1.5-mile loop trail); **Barker Dam** (an easy 1.3-mile loop where you might see bighorn sheep); and the sublime **Oasis of Mara**, an 0.5-mile stroll behind the visitor center of the same name.

Sunset is a no-brainer: **Keys View** (Keys View Rd., 20 minutes off Park Blvd.), an overlook at 5,100 feet, gives you a view westward across Coachella Valley—particularly stunning when the sun dips behind the snow-covered San Jacinto Mountains. Bring your camera, tripod, and binoculars: It's worth the trouble,

Joshua Tree National Park, CA

especially to capture iconic Joshua trees in the foreground of those burnished desert sunsets.

Museum. Head down to **Keys Ranch**, built by ranchers and homesteaders Bill and Frances Keys. They raised five children, planted an orchard, built several structures, and lived on-site for 60 years until 1969. Ranch tours, the only way to see this spectacular piece of desert history, require tickets that you purchase at the Oasis of Mara Visitor Center on the morning of the tour.

Programs & Activities. Joshua Tree's ranger-led programs mesh perfectly with what the park is all about. They include the **Joshua Tree Rocks!** geology walk (1 mile, near Skull Rock), an **oasis walk** (easy 0.5-mile stroll from the Oasis of Mara Visitor Center), the **I Speak for the Trees** walk (easy 0.4-mile walk along the Cap Rock Nature Trail), and the more strenuous, steep 3-mile hike to **Mastodon Peak**.

After sunset, you can appreciate the spectacular, star-filled skies that have made Joshua Tree a designated International Dark Sky Park. The **Night Sky Festival**, usually held in early November, features free talks and solar viewing by day and astronomy programs by night. The park's geology makes it a favorite destination for rock climbing; **Joshua Tree Rock Climbing School** (760/366-4745, www.joshuatreerockclimbing.com) offers courses for all levels. Joshua Tree's backcountry roads and trails are also perfect for **mountain biking** and **horseback riding**.

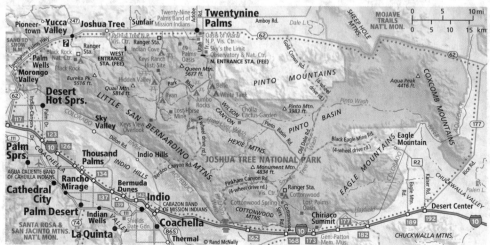

Atlas map **p. 9, J-9**

ZION NATIONAL PARK
UTAH

Burnished red Navajo sandstone cliffs rise from the Colorado Plateau, forming a series of majestic outcroppings illuminated by the sun amid a deep-blue Utah sky. Zion Canyon, one of this park's most striking formations, features 2,000-foot-high walls carved over millennia by the snaking Virgin River. On any given day, thousands of people gaze up at the canyon's walls and its intrepid rock climbers.

1. The Narrows. **2.** Hiking in Zion. **3.** Sandstone landscape.

GETTING ORIENTED

Zion is in southwestern Utah, near the Nevada and Arizona borders. Las Vegas' McCarran International Airport is 160 miles southwest of the South Entrance, mainly via I-15; Salt Lake City International Airport is 313 miles northeast, also via I-15. It's 40 miles on UT 9 and I-15 between the South Entrance and the less-trafficked, northwestern Kolob Canyons Entrance. The even quieter East Entrance, on UT 9, accesses the scenic Zion–Mount Carmel Highway.

In-park lodging is limited to camping (Recreation.gov). Motels and inns line UT 9 in Springdale and Rockville (www.zionpark.com for both). St. George (www.visitstgeorge.com), 41 miles west of the South Entrance, and Kanab (www.visitsouthernutah.com), 40 miles east, are also good bases for exploring Zion as well as Bryce Canyon and the Grand Canyon's North Rim. **Park Contact Info:** *435/772-3256, www.nps.gov/zion.*

Atlas map **p. 50, I-2**

PARK HIGHLIGHTS

Natural Attractions. With more than 4 million visitors annually, Zion is one of America's most popular national parks. (It has even considered introducing an online reservation system to address overcrowding and potential environmental damage.) It's wise to book in-park campsites and rooms at nearby hotels well in advance.

The sheer walls of Zion Canyon and many other mesas, buttes, and rusty red outcroppings are the park's main draws. You can see formations like the Court of the Patriarchs and Weeping Rock as you move in to the canyon, and it's impossible to say whether the canyon itself is more spectacular seen from its floor looking up or from its top looking down.

Zion displays a more desert-style landscape in its southwest corner (accessible by two trailheads off UT 9); the varied landscape of the high-elevation Kolob Canyons area in the northwest, however, is worth a full extra day. Few explore Kolob's hikes and views or the stunning 287-foot span of Kolob Arch, a strenuous 14-mile (round-trip)

Zion National Park, UT

hike that is one of the park's hidden treasures.

Trails, Drives & Viewpoints.

The 7-mile (one-way) Zion Canyon Scenic Drive from the South Entrance visitor center, which ends at the natural amphitheater called the Temple of Sinawava, and the 12-mile (one-way) Zion–Mount Carmel Highway, connecting the park's South Entrance to the East Entrance, are unmissable. Zion Canyon can be visited only via park shuttle bus mid-March through October (and weekends in November), but the spectacular narrowing and rising of the canyon's walls inspires awe as you travel farther in. The winding Zion–Mount Carmel Highway is one of America's most beautiful roads, with striated mesas and canyon views.

The Narrows begin at the north end of Zion Canyon; here, the canyon's walls are sometimes only 20 or 30 feet wide. The easy 2.2-mile round-trip Riverside Walk Trail is where you can examine The Narrows for yourself. For a spectacular bird's-eye view of Zion Canyon, the strenuous, 5.4-mile round-trip Angels Landing Trail from the Grotto trailhead, with its cliff-hugging stone steps and helpful (and necessary) chain handholds, is one of Zion's greatest experiences.

Programs & Activities. Rangers lead a great mix of summer programs, including a moderate 2.5-hour, 3.3-mile round-trip hike on the Watchman Trail that climbs to a great view of Zion Canyon. In mornings and afternoons, rangers conduct Patio Talks on wildlife and geology; evening programs generally feature more personal stories.

Zion Canyon Scenic Drive is open for cycling, as is the pedestrian-and-bike-only Pa'rus Trail (3.5 miles round-trip). Zion Canyon's sheer cliffs and narrow slot canyons draw thousands for climbing every year, and canyoneering (a combination of climbing, rappelling, and scrambling) is becoming increasingly popular. Permits for canyoneering and overnight climbs are required.

ROCKY MOUNTAIN NATIONAL PARK
COLORADO

Studded by peaks soaring majestically above the timberline, this north-central Colorado park is marked by a treeless ecosystem that's home to some of Earth's hardiest living things. The wide swath of high-country alpine tundra is largely dormant for half the year as snow falls, winds howl, and temperatures plunge. In warmer months, low-country forests, verdant meadows, and shimmering lakes and rivers define the landscape of this hiker's paradise.

1. A Rocky Mountain National Park vista. **2.** Alberta Falls. **3.** Elk.

GETTING ORIENTED

Rocky Mountain is 40 miles northwest of Boulder via US 36 and 35 miles west of Loveland via US 34. Denver International Airport is 78 miles southeast of the **Beaver Meadows Visitor Center**. The largest of the park's five campgrounds (Recreation.gov) is near the **Moraine Park Discovery Center**, 2 miles southwest of Beaver Meadows.

Amenities-filled gateway towns include **Estes Park** (www.visitestespark.com)—3 miles east of Beaver Meadows and 4 miles southeast of the **Fall River Visitor Center**—and **Grand Lake** (grandlakechamber.com), 2 miles south of the **Kawuneeche Visitor Center**. Trail Ridge Road (closed late Oct.–June) runs 48 miles between Estes Park and Grand Lake. **Alpine Visitor Center**, near Trail Ridge Road's high point (12,183 feet), is 22 miles west of Beaver Meadows. **Park Contact Info:** *970/586-1206, www.nps.gov/romo.*

PARK HIGHLIGHTS

Natural Attractions. Although the park is home to elk, black bears, and mountain lions, the star attractions are its namesake **Rocky Mountains**. Their formation began about 70 million years ago, when geologic uplift began pushing ancient rocks about a mile skyward. Of the park's 124 named peaks, 20 have summits higher than 13,000 feet. At 14,259 feet, **Longs Peak** is the tallest, and a draw for climbers from all over the world.

Subalpine forests and meadows dominate the mountains' lower flanks. Pine beetles, insects the size of a grain of rice that kill trees by feasting inside the bark, have ravaged many of the forests. Above 11,000 feet, woods and meadows give way to alpine tundra, which makes up more than a third of the park's land area. Windswept and devoid of trees, this fragile ecosystem typically sees at least a little snowfall every month of the year.

Trails, Drives & Viewpoints. Rocky Mountain has more than 300 miles of trails. The easy, 0.6-mile loop around **Bear Lake** is a good scenic introduction to the east side. From the **Glacier Gorge trailhead** nearby, it's a moderate 0.6 miles to Alberta Falls and a moderate 2.8 miles to Mills Lake.

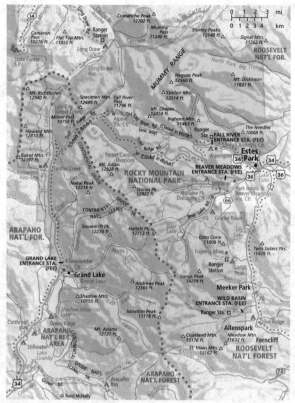

Atlas map **p. 12, B-5**

In the Wild Basin Unit, the **Ouzel Falls Trail** offers a moderate, 5.4-mile round-trip to a waterfall named for the bird also known as the American dipper. Just north of Grand Lake, the **North Inlet Trail** is a moderate, 6.8-mile round-trip to Cascade Falls by way of a wide mountain valley; more experienced hikers can continue to a pair of lakes and Flattop Mountain.

Twisting, turning, and gaining more than 3,000 feet along its 48 miles, the seasonally open **Trail Ridge Road** ranks among the highest and most scenic roads in the United States. Numerous endless-view overlooks merit a stop, including Far View Curve and Rainbow Curve. **Old Fall River Road**, the park's original automobile route, is a curving one-way, 11-mile drive that connects with Trail Ridge Road; it has been called "a motor nature trail."

Museums & Sites. On Rocky Mountain's west side, **Holzwarth Historic Site** was homesteaded in 1917 and later became a dude ranch. It's open for guided tours. The area also has a mining legacy: Reachable by a 2.8-mile hike from the Longs Peak Trailhead on the park's east side, **Eugenia Mine** was

Rocky Mountain National Park, CO

abandoned in 1919 but has intriguing ruins. The remains of **Lulu City**, a mining boomtown that went bust in the 1880s, are 3.7 miles from the Colorado River Trailhead near Grand Lake.

Programs & Activities. In summer, ranger-led activities include guided hikes, talks on ecology and geology, and stargazing programs. Guided snowshoe walks are available in winter. **Horseback riding** is a staple, and the park has two stables: **Glacier Creek** (970/586-3244, www.sombrero.com) and **Moraine Park** (970/586-2327, www.sombrero.com).

Climbers flock to Longs Peak and other mountains. The **Colorado Mountain School** (341 Moraine Ave., Estes Park, 720/387-8944, coloradomountainschool.com) offers guided **mountaineering** and **climbing** expeditions.

GATEWAY ARCH NATIONAL PARK
MISSOURI

America's newest national park is also its smallest. As the saying goes, though, "Big things come in small packages." And this package contains the country's tallest manmade monument, an iconic structure that memorializes a whole lot of history. Rising 630 feet and framing the dome of the Old Courthouse, also part of the park, the Arch was completed in the late 1960s—a Mid-Century metaphor for manifest destiny ideals.

1. Downtown St. Louis skyline. **2.** Old Courthouse. **3.** Gateway Arch grounds in spring.

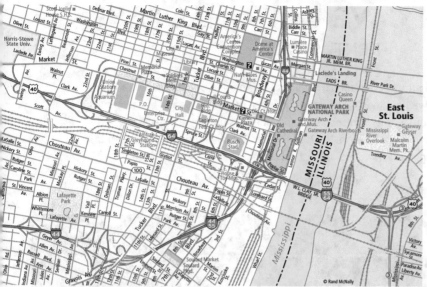

Atlas map **p. 28, C-7**

Gateway Arch National Park, MO

GETTING ORIENTED

Gateway Arch is edged by **St. Louis** (explorestlouis.com) on one side and the Mississippi River (across from East St. Louis in Illinois) on the other. Interstate 44 cuts through the park between downtown and the river. A pedestrian-friendly land bridge connects the Old Courthouse with the Arch and its grounds. North of downtown, I-70 runs to I-44 from the west—including the 15 miles from St. Louis Lambert International Airport—as well as from the east. In the south, I-64, I-44, or I-55 get you to the park.

Numerous downtown hotels and public parking lots are within walking distance. **Metro system** (www.metrostlouis.org) buses—including hop-on-hop-off #99 Downtown Trolley—and trains serve both Missouri and Illinois. **Park Contact Info: *314/655-1600 (recorded info), 877/982-1410 (to buy timed-entry tickets), www.nps.gov/jeff.***

PARK HIGHLIGHTS

Viewpoints. Plenty of national parks feature spectacular views as part of a visit. Here, though, the views are arguably *the* reason to visit. One bank of windows atop the 630-foot **Arch** looks across the Mississippi River and into Illinois. Windows on the other side take in the west as far as the eye can see, which, on a clear day, is roughly 30 miles.

To experience the park's recently refurbished glory and classic vistas, purchase timed-entry, **Journey to the Top** tickets for 4-minute tram rides up well in advance through **GatewayArch. com**, the park's concessionaire partner. Although the tram system accommodates up to 6,400 visitors daily, tickets can sell out. Also, arrive at least 30 minutes early to allow time for airport-style security screening. Stay in the observation area as long as you like; trams for the 3-minute ride down depart every 10 minutes or so. Note, though, that there are no restrooms or other facilities at the top; plan accordingly.

If you prefer to stay grounded, you can check out top-side views on live web cams; see the documentary *Monument to the Dream*, covering the Arch's construction and significance; and visit the underground Museum of the Gateway Arch (formerly the Museum of Westward Expansion).

History, Museums & Activities. Some people wonder why this very small, very urban site was made a national park in 2018. To be fair, the National Park Service has always overseen it, and it does commemorate a pioneering history without which there might be fewer vast, wild spaces farther west for the park service to protect.

Established in 1935 by President Franklin Roosevelt as the Jefferson National Expansion Memorial, the site honors not only Thomas Jefferson's vision

of westward expansion but also the Louisiana Purchase and the Lewis & Clark Expedition.

It was just northwest of St. Louis, where the Mississippi and Missouri rivers meet, that the Corps of Discovery began its 1804–06 journey across uncharted territory to the Pacific. The onset of World War II and other issues delayed the memorial's development. In 1947–48, a design competition was held, and Eero Saarinen's concrete and stainless-steel Arch won out over 172 other entries, including one by his father, Eliel.

Six refurbished galleries in the **Museum of the Gateway Arch** look back across all this history using very forward-facing technology. Video and other interactive displays cover the Native American and Creole cultures of early St. Louis; Jefferson's vision for westward expansion; the steamboats, railroads, and other industries that helped to propel expansion; and the building of the Arch itself.

Two historic legal cases are highlighted on the daily, 45-minute, ranger-led tours of the **Old Courthouse**: The landmark Dredd Scott Case, involving emancipation and heard here in 1847 and 1850 (before a U.S. Supreme Court decision in 1857), and the 1870 case of Virginia Minor, a suffragette who sued for the right to vote.

For a leisurely park experience, board a replica 19th-century steamboat for a one-hour **riverboat cruise** (GatewayArch. com) with fantastic views of the Arch from Old Muddy. For a more active approach, look into biking, in-line-skating, or walking/running along the paved, 11-mile **St. Louis Riverfront Trail** (www.traillink.com).

MAMMOTH CAVE NATIONAL PARK
KENTUCKY

On the surface, it looks as if Mammoth Cave National Park has little to offer, but its 586,000 annual visitors are drawn by what's below: more than 400 surveyed miles of passageways and chambers. Even in the 19th century, Mammoth was recognized as one of America's natural wonders, a reputation that would grow with the cave itself. In 1972, spelunkers discovered that it connected to a neighboring network, establishing it as the world's longest cave system.

1. Cave entrance. **2.** Autumn at Mammoth Cave National Park. **3.** Cave interior, Frozen Niagara section.

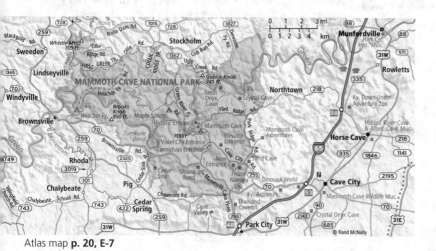

Atlas map **p. 20, E-7**

Mammoth Cave National Park, KY

GETTING ORIENTED

Mammoth Cave is in south-central Kentucky. Louisville Muhammad Ali International Airport is 85 miles north of the park entrance, and Tennessee's Nashville International is 95 miles south. From Louisville, take I-65 south to Exit 53 in Cave City; from Nashville, take I-65 north to Exit 48 in Park City. Mammoth Cave is 28 miles northeast of Bowling Green via I-65.

In the park's main visitor area, a pedestrian bridge connects the visitor center to the Lodge at Mammoth Cave (171 Hotel Rd., 844/760-2283, mammothcavelodge.com); the main cave entrance is just down the hill. Nearby towns with lodging and other amenities include Cave City (cavecity.com), Park City, and Bowling Green (www. visitbgky.com). The park also has three campgrounds (Recreation.gov). **Park Contact Info: *270/758-2180, www.nps. gov/maca.***

PARK HIGHLIGHTS

Cave Tours. You need to take a tour to see the cave. The roster of offerings changes seasonally, with tours lasting from 75 minutes to 6 hours and prices varying accordingly. Sign up in advance if possible since tours sell out quickly, especially in summer. Some tours enter at the Historic Entrance (aka Natural Entrance) by the visitor center; others require a 10-minute bus ride to the New Entrance.

Among the easiest and most popular is the 75-minute Frozen Niagara Tour

highlighting stalactites, stalagmites, flowstones, and Frozen Niagara itself, a formation that looks like a freeze-dried waterfall. Going deeper into the cave, the moderate, 2-hour Domes and Dripstones Tour descends nearly 300 steps to dazzling domes, pits, and dripstone formations before returning to sights seen on the Frozen Niagara Tour.

The moderate, 2-hour Historic Tour uses the Historic Entrance and leads to places familiar to visitors in the 1800s, including the Rotunda, Broadway, and Fat Man's Misery. Designed for people who use a walker or wheelchair, the 2-hour Mammoth Cave Accessible Tour visits unique gypsum formations, historical cave writing, and the Snowball Room, where gypsum nodules cover the ceiling.

Specialty cave tours supplement regularly scheduled tours and explore the cave in different ways. The strenuous, 4-mile Violet City Lantern Tour visits the cave Tom Sawyer–style: you carry a flickering lantern. A handful of "wild" tours, including the very strenuous, 5-mile Wild Cave Tour, are for those who can handle tight spaces and don't mind getting dirty. This one finds you donning gloves, knee pads, and a helmet as you walk, kneel, crouch, and crawl your way through the cave.

Trails & Viewpoints. More than 80 miles of trails fan out across the park, with the easiest and most accessible being the 7 miles of routes that surround the visitor center. On these you can see the Green River, walk along ridges that provide lovely views of Doyle Valley, and trek beside huge depressions caused by sinkholes.

The easy, 0.75-mile Heritage Trail passes the Old Guides Cemetery, where you can see the grave of cave explorer Stephen Bishop, a mixed-race slave who, in the mid-19th century, navigated uncharted passages to create detailed cave maps. A popular 9-mile path adjacent to an old railroad bed, the Mammoth Cave Railroad Bike and Hike Trail runs from the visitor center to Park City and accommodates bicyclists, pedestrians, joggers, and dogs on a leash. Hybrid bikes can handle the hard-packed gravel.

Programs & Activities. Outside the cave, rangers host free "surface" talks and presentations that vary by season. In summer, evening presentations are held nightly in the Amphitheater (less often in other seasons), highlighting topics related to Mammoth Cave. There are short Porch Talks about the park's cultural heritage; a 45-minute Heritage Walk explaining Mammoth Cave Estate and the Old Guides Cemetery; and a 45-minute Sloans Pond Crossing Walk. Mammoth Cave is along the Mississippi Flyway, and rangers host two-hour birding excursions.

Road through the park

Tourism Contacts

On the road or before you go, log on to the official tourism website of your destination. These websites offer terrific ideas about organizing a visit and often include calendars of special events and activities. Prefer calling? Most states offer toll-free numbers.

UNITED STATES

Alabama Tourism Department
(800) 252-2262
(334) 242-4169
tourism.alabama.gov

Alaska Tourism
www.travelalaska.com

Arizona Office of Tourism
(866) 275-5816
(602) 364-3700
www.visitarizona.com
tourism.az.gov

Arkansas Department of Parks & Tourism
(501) 682-7777
www.arkansas.com

California Tourism
(877) 225-4367
(916) 444-4429
www.visitcalifornia.com

Colorado Tourism Office
(800) 265-6723
www.colorado.com

Connecticut Office of Tourism
(888) 288-4748
(860) 500-2300
www.ctvisit.com

Delaware Tourism Office
(866) 284-7483
www.visitdelaware.com

Visit Florida
(888) 735-2872
(850) 488-5607
www.visitflorida.com

Explore Georgia
(800) 847-4842
www.exploregeorgia.org

Hawaii Visitors & Convention Bureau
(800) 464-2924
www.gohawaii.com

Idaho Tourism
(800) 847-4843
(208) 334-2470
visitidaho.org

Illinois Office of Tourism
(800) 226-6632
(312) 814-4732
www.enjoyillinois.com

Indiana Office of Tourism Development
(800) 677-9800
visitindiana.com

Iowa Tourism Office
(800) 345-4692
www.traveliowa.com

Kansas Tourism Office
(785) 296-2009
www.travelks.com

Kentucky Department of Tourism
(800) 225-8747
(502) 564-4930
www.kentuckytourism.com

Louisiana Office of Tourism
(800) 677-4082
(225) 635-0090
www.louisianatravel.com

Maine Office of Tourism
(888) 624-6345
(207) 624-7483
visitmaine.com

Maryland Office of Tourism Development
(866) 639-3526
www.visitmaryland.org

Massachusetts Office of Travel & Tourism
(800) 227-6277
(617) 973-8500
www.massvacation.com

Pure Michigan
(888) 784-7328
www.michigan.org

Explore Minnesota
(888) 847-4866
(651) 556-8465
www.exploreminnesota.com

Visit Mississippi
(866) 733-6477
(601) 359-3297
visitmississippi.org

Missouri Division of Tourism
(573) 751-4133
www.visitmo.com

Montana Office of Tourism
(800) 847-4868
www.visitmt.com

Nebraska Tourism Commission
(402) 471-3796
(877) 632-7275
visitnebraska.com

Travel Nevada
(800) 638-2328
(775) 687-4322
travelnevada.com

New Hampshire Division of Travel and Tourism Development
(603) 271-2665
www.visitnh.gov

New Jersey Division of Travel and Tourism
(609) 599-6540
www.visitnj.org

New Mexico Tourism Department
(505) 827-7336
www.newmexico.org

New York State Division of Tourism
(800) 225-5697
www.iloveny.com

Visit North Carolina
(800) 847-4862
www.visitnc.com

North Dakota Tourism Division
(800) 435-5663
(701) 328-2525
www.ndtourism.com

Tourism Ohio
(800) 282-5393
www.ohio.org

Oklahoma Tourism Department
(800) 652-6552
www.travelok.com

Travel Oregon
(800) 547-7842
traveloregon.com

Visit PA
(800) 847-4872
visitpa.com

Rhode Island Tourism Division
(800) 556-2484
www.visitrhodeisland.com

South Carolina Department of Parks, Recreation and Tourism
(803) 734-0124
discoversouthcarolina.com

South Dakota Department of Tourism
(800) 732-5682
www.travelsouthdakota.com

Tennessee Department of Tourist Development
(615) 741-2159
www.tnvacation.com

Texas Tourism
(800) 452-9292
www.traveltexas.com

Visit Utah
(800) 200-1160
(801) 538-1900
www.visitutah.com

Vermont Department of Tourism & Marketing
(802) 828-3237
(800) 837-6668
www.vermontvacation.com

Virginia Tourism Corporation
(800) 847-4882
www.virginia.org

Washington Tourism Alliance
(800) 544-1800
www.experiencewa.com

Destination DC
(202) 789-7000
washington.org

West Virginia Tourism Office
(800) 225-5982
(304) 558-2200
wvtourism.com

Wisconsin Department of Tourism
(800) 432-8747
(608) 266-2161
www.travelwisconsin.com

Wyoming Office of Tourism
(800) 225-5996
(307) 777-7777
www.wyomingtourism.org

CANADA

Travel Alberta
(800) 252-3782
www.travelalberta.com

Destination British Columbia
(800) 822-7899
(604) 660-2861
www.hellobc.com

Travel Manitoba
(800) 665-0040
(204) 927-7800
www.travelmanitoba.com

Tourism New Brunswick
(800) 561-0123
www.tourismnewbrunswick.ca

Newfoundland and Labrador Tourism
(800) 563-6353
(709) 729-2830
www.newfoundlandlabrador.com

Northwest Territories Tourism
(800) 661-0788
(867) 873-5007
spectacularnwt.com

Tourism Nova Scotia
(800) 565-0000
(902) 742-0511
www.novascotia.com

Ontario Tourism Marketing Partnership Corporation
(800) 668-2746
www.ontariotravel.net

Prince Edward Island Tourism
(800) 463-4734
(902) 437-8570
www.tourismpei.com

Tourisme Québec
(877) 266-5687
(514) 873-2015
www.quebecoriginal.com

Tourism Saskatchewan
(877) 237-2273
(306) 787-9600
www.tourismsaskatchewan.com
www.sasktourism.com

Yukon Department of Tourism & Culture
(800) 661-0494
www.travelyukon.com

MEXICO

Mexico Tourism Board
(800) 262-9128
www.visitmexico.com/en

PUERTO RICO

Discover Puerto Rico
(800) 866-7827
(787) 721-2400
www.discoverpuertorico.com
prtourism.com

UNITED STATES VIRGIN ISLANDS

Visit USVI
(800) 372-8784
www.visitusvi.com

Road Work

Road construction and road conditions resources

Get the Info from the 511 hotline

The U.S. Federal Highway Administration has begun implementing a national system of highway and road conditions/construction information for travelers. Under the new plan, travelers can dial 511 and get up-to-date information on roads and highways.

Implementation of 511 is the responsibility of state and local agencies.

For more details, visit: www.fhwa.dot.gov/trafficinfo/511.htm.

UNITED STATES

Alabama
(888) 588-2848
algotraffic.com
www.dot.state.al.us

Alaska
511
(866) 282-7577
511.alaska.gov
www.dot.state.ak.us

Arizona
511
(888) 411-7623
www.az511.com
www.azdot.gov

Arkansas
(800) 245-1672
(501) 569-2227
www.idrivearkansas.com
www.arkansashighways.com

California
www.dot.ca.gov
Eastern Sierras District 9:
511, (800) 427-7623
www.dot.ca.gov/d9
Inland Empire:
511, (877) 694-3511
www.ie511.org
Los Angeles metro area:
511, (877) 224-6511
go511.com
Sacramento Region:
511, (877) 511-8747
www.sacregion511.org
San Diego area:
511, (855) 467-3511
www.511sd.com
San Francisco Bay area:
511, (888) 500-4626
511.org
San Luis Obispo area:
511, (866) 928-8923

Colorado
511
(303) 639-1111
www.cotrip.org
www.codot.gov

Connecticut
(860) 594-2650
(860) 594-2000
cttravelsmart.org
www.ct.gov/dot

Delaware
(800) 652-5600
(302) 760-2080
www.deldot.gov

Florida
511
(866) 511-3352
fl511.com
fdot.gov

Georgia
511
(877) 694-2511
www.511ga.org

Hawaii
(808) 587-2220
hidot.hawaii.gov
Honolulu & Oahu:
511
www.goakamai.org

Idaho
511
(888) 432-7623
www.511.idaho.gov
www.itd.idaho.gov

Illinois
(800) 452-4368
www.gettingaroundillinois.com
www.dot.il.gov

Indiana
(800) 261-7623
(855) 463-6848
www.in.gov/indot/2420.htm
indot.carsprogram.org

Iowa
511
(800) 288-1047
www.511ia.org
www.iowadot.gov

Kansas
511
(866) 511-5368
www.kandrive.org
www.ksdot.org

Kentucky
511
(866) 737-3767
drive.ky.gov
transportation.ky.gov

Louisiana
511
(888) 762-3511
www.511la.org
www.dotd.la.gov

Maine
511
(207) 624-3000
newengland511.org
www.maine.gov/mdot

Maryland
511
(855) 466-3511
(410) 582-5650
www.md511.org
www.roads.maryland.gov

Massachusetts
511
Metro Boston: (617) 986-5511
Central: (508) 499-5511
Western: (413) 754-5511
www.mass511.com

Michigan
(517) 373-2090
www.michigan.gov/drive
www.michigan.gov/mdot

Minnesota
511
(800) 542-0220
(651) 296-3000
(800) 657-3774
www.511mn.org
www.dot.state.mn.us

Mississippi
511
(888) 672-4502
www.mdottraffic.com

Missouri
(888) 275-6636
(573) 751-2551
www.modot.org
traveler.modot.org/map

Montana
511
(800) 226-7623
(406) 444-6200
www.mdt.mt.gov/travinfo

Nebraska
511
(800) 906-9069
(402) 471-4567
www.511.nebraska.gov
www.dot.nebraska.gov

Nevada
511
(877) 687-6237
(775) 888-7000
nvroads.com/511-home
www.nevadadot.com

New Hampshire
(603) 271-6862
newengland511.org
www.nhtmc.com

New Jersey
511
(866) 511-6538
www.511nj.org
www.state.nj.us/transportation

New Mexico
511
(800) 432-4269
(505) 827-5100
www.nmroads.com
www.dot.state.nm.us

New York
511
(888) 465-1169
(877) 690-5110
511ny.org
www.dot.ny.gov
New York State Thruway:
(800) 847-8929
www.thruway.ny.gov

North Carolina
511
(877) 511-4662
www.ncdot.gov/travel-maps
www.ncdot.gov

North Dakota
511
(866) 696-3511
www.dot.nd.gov/travel
www.dot.nd.gov/travel-info-v2

Ohio
511
(855) 511-6446
www.ohgo.com
www.dot.state.oh.us
Ohio Turnpike:
(440) 234-2081
www.ohioturnpike.org

Oklahoma
(844) 465-4997
(405) 522-2800
okroads.org
www.okladot.state.ok.us

Oregon
511
(800) 977-6368
(503) 588-2941
(888) 275-6368
www.tripcheck.com
www.oregon.gov/odot

Pennsylvania
511
(877) 511-7366
www.511pa.com
www.penndot.gov

Rhode Island
(888) 401-4511
(401) 222-2450
www.dot.ri.gov/travel

South Carolina
511
(877) 511-4672
(855) 467-2368
www.511sc.org
www.scdot.org

South Dakota
511
(866) 697-3511
www.sddot.com
www.safetravelusa.com/sd

Tennessee
511
(877) 244-0065
smartway.tn.gov
www.tn.gov/tdot/welcome-to-tennessee-511

Texas
(800) 452-9292
(877) 511-3255 (Dallas/Ft. Worth)
(512) 463-8588
www.drivetexas.org
www.txdot.gov

Utah
511
(866) 511-8824
(801) 887-3700
(801) 965-4000
www.udot.utah.gov
www.utahcommuterlink.com

Vermont
newengland511.org
www.vtrans.vermont.gov

Virginia
511
(866) 695-1182
(800) 578-4111
(800) 367-7623
www.511virginia.org
www.virginiadot.org/travel

Washington
511
(800) 695-7623
www.wsdot.com/traffic

Washington, D.C.
311
(202) 673-6813
ddot.dc.gov

West Virginia
511
(855) 699-8511
www.wv511.org
transportation.wv.gov

Wisconsin
511
(866) 511-9472
511wi.gov

Wyoming
511
(888) 996-7623
www.wyoroad.info

CANADA

Alberta
511
(855) 391-9743
511.alberta.ca

British Columbia
(800) 550-4997
www.drivebc.ca
www2.gov.bc.ca/gov/content/transportation

Manitoba
511
(877) 627-6237 (in MB, SK, ON, and North Dakota)
www.manitoba511.ca/en

New Brunswick
511
(800) 561-4063
(506) 453-3939
www.gnb.ca/roads

Newfoundland & Labrador
(709) 729-2300
www.roads.gov.nl.ca

Northwest Territories
www.dot.gov.nt.ca/Highways/Highway-Conditions

Nova Scotia
511
In Canada, outside NS:
(888) 780-4440
(902) 424-3933
511.novascotia.ca

Ontario
511
(800) 268-4686
Toronto area: (416) 235-4686
511on.ca
www.mto.gov.on.ca/english/traveller

Prince Edward Island
511
In Canada outside PEI:
(855) 241-2680
(902) 368-4770
511.gov.pe.ca/en

Québec
511
(888) 355-0511
www.quebec511.info/en

Saskatchewan
(888) 335-7623
Saskatoon area: (306) 933-8333
Regina area: (306) 787-7623
www.saskatchewan.ca/residents/transportation/highways/highway-hotline

Yukon Territory
511
www.511yukon.ca

MEXICO

www.gob.mx/carreteras

PUERTO RICO

(800) 981-3021
(787) 977-2200
its.dtop.gov.pr/en
www.dtop.gov.pr/carretera

© Rand McNally

National Monuments and Memorials

1M Agate Fossil Beds	E-6
2M Alibates Flint Quarries	G-6
3M Admiralty Island	J-4
4M Agua Fria	G-3
5M Aniakchak	J-3
6M Aztec Ruins	F-4
7M Bandelier	F-4
8M Bears Ears	F-4
9M Berryessa Snow Mountain	D-1
10M Browns Canyon	F-5
11M Cabrillo	G-2
12M Canyon de Chelly	F-4
13M Cape Krusenstern	I-3
14M Capulin Volcano	F-6
15M Casa Grande Ruins	F-3
16M Castillo de San Marcos	H-12
17M Cedar Breaks	F-3
18M Chiricahua	H-4
19M Colorado	E-5
20M Craters of the Moon	D-4
21M Devils Tower	D-6
22M Dinosaur	E-5
23M Effigy Mounds	D-9
24M El Malpais	G-4
25M El Morro	G-4
26M Florissant Fossil Beds	E-5
27M Fort Clatsop	B-2
28M Fort Frederica	H-12
29M Fort Matanzas	H-12
30M Fort Monroe	F-13
31M Fort Ord	E-1
32M Fort Pulaski	H-12
33M Fort Sumter	G-12
34M Fort Union	G-5
35M Fort Butte	D-4
36M George Washington Carver	F-8
37M Giant Sequoia	F-2
38M Gila Cliff Dwellings	G-4
39M Gold Butte	F-3
40M Grand Canyon-Parashant	F-3
41M Grand Portage	C-9
42M Grand Staircase-Escalante	F-3
43M Hagerman Fossil Beds	D-3
44M Homestead	E-8
45M Hovenweep	F-4
46M Jewel Cave	D-6
47M Katahdin Woods and Waters	B-14
48M Lava Beds	D-2
49M Mojave Trails	F-2
50M Montezuma Castle	G-4
51M Mount Rushmore	D-6
52M Mount St. Helens	B-2
53M Navajo	F-4
54M Newberry Volcanic	C-2
55M Ocmulgee	G-11
56M Organ Mountains-Desert Peaks	H-5
57M Organ Pipe Cactus	G-3
58M Petroglyph	G-5
59M Pipe Spring	F-3
60M Pipestone	D-8
61M Rainbow Bridge	F-3
62M Rio Grande del Norte	F-5
63M Russell Cave	G-11
64M Salinas Pueblo Missions	G-5
65M San Gabriel Mountains	F-2
66M Sand to Snow	F-2
67M Santa Rosa and San Jacinto Mountains	G-2
68M Scotts Bluff	E-6
69M Sonoran Desert	G-3
70M Sunset Crater Volcano	F-4
71M Timpanogos Cave	E-4
72M Tonto	G-3
73M Tuzigoot	G-3
74M Upper Missouri River Breaks	B-5
75M Vermilion Cliffs	F-4
76M White Sands	F-5
77M Wright Brothers	F-13
78M Wupatki	F-4

National Parks

1P Acadia	C-14	20P Glacier Bay	J-4	40P Mesa Verde	F-5
2P Arches	E-4	21P Glacier	B-4	41P Mt. Rainier	B-3
3P Badlands	D-6	22P Grand Canyon	F-3	42P North Cascades	B-3
4P Big Bend	I-6	23P Grand Teton	D-4	43P Olympic	B-3
5P Biscayne	J-13	24P Great Basin	E-3	44P Petrified Forest	G-4
6P Black Canyon	F-5	25P Great Sand Dunes	F-5	45P Pinnacles	E-1
7P Bryce Canyon	F-3	26P Great Smoky Mtns.	G-11	46P Redwood	C-1
8P Canyonlands	E-4	27P Guadalupe Mtns.	H-5	47P Rocky Mountain	E-5
9P Capitol Reef	E-4	28P Haleakala	I-2	48P Saguaro	H-4
10P Carlsbad Caverns	H-5	29P Hawai'i Volcanoes	I-2	49P Sequoia	F-2
11P Channel Islands	F-1	30P Hot Springs	G-9	50P Shenandoah	E-12
12P Congaree	G-12	31P Isle Royale	C-9	51P Theodore Roosevelt	C-6
13P Crater Lake	C-2	32P Joshua Tree	F-2	52P Voyageurs	C-8
14P Cuyahoga Valley	E-11	33P Katmai	J-3	53P Wind Cave	D-6
15P Death Valley	F-2	34P Kenai Fjords	J-3	54P Wrangell-St. Elias	I-4
16P Denali	I-3	35P Kings Canyon	E-2	55P Yellowstone	C-5
17P Dry Tortugas	J-12	36P Kobuk Valley	I-3	56P Yosemite	E-2
18P Everglades	J-13	37P Lake Clark	J-3	57P Zion	F-3
19P Gates of the Arctic	I-3	38P Lassen Volcanic	D-2		
		39P Mammoth Cave	F-10		

Alabama

Population: 4,779,736
Land Area: 50,645 sq. mi.
Capital: Montgomery

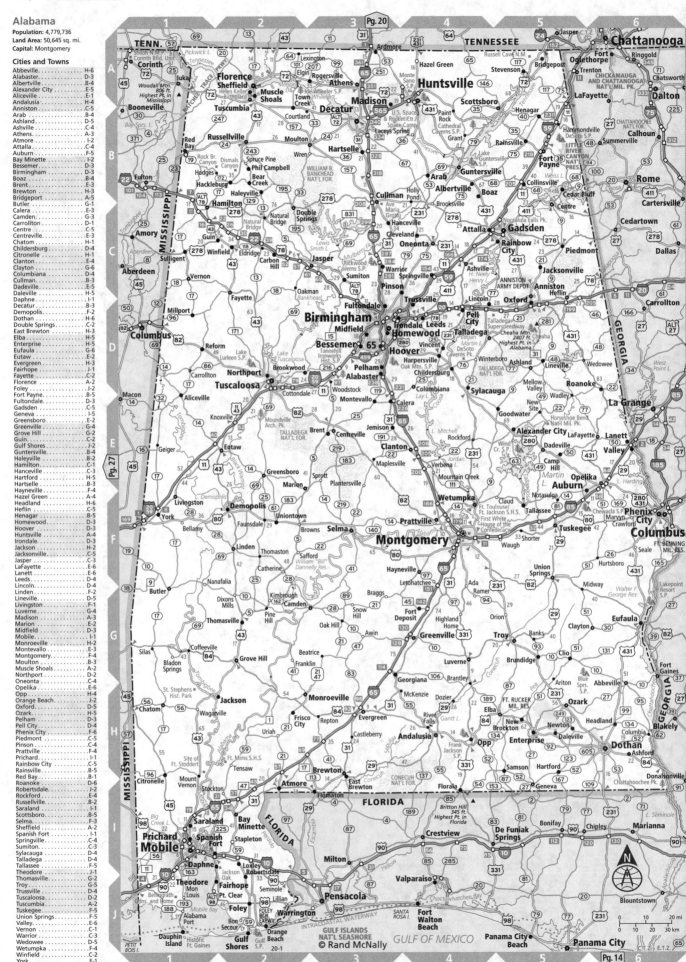

Pg. 20

Pg. 14

Pg. 27

NOTE: Maps are not always in alphabetical order.
See Page 1 for map location in this atlas.

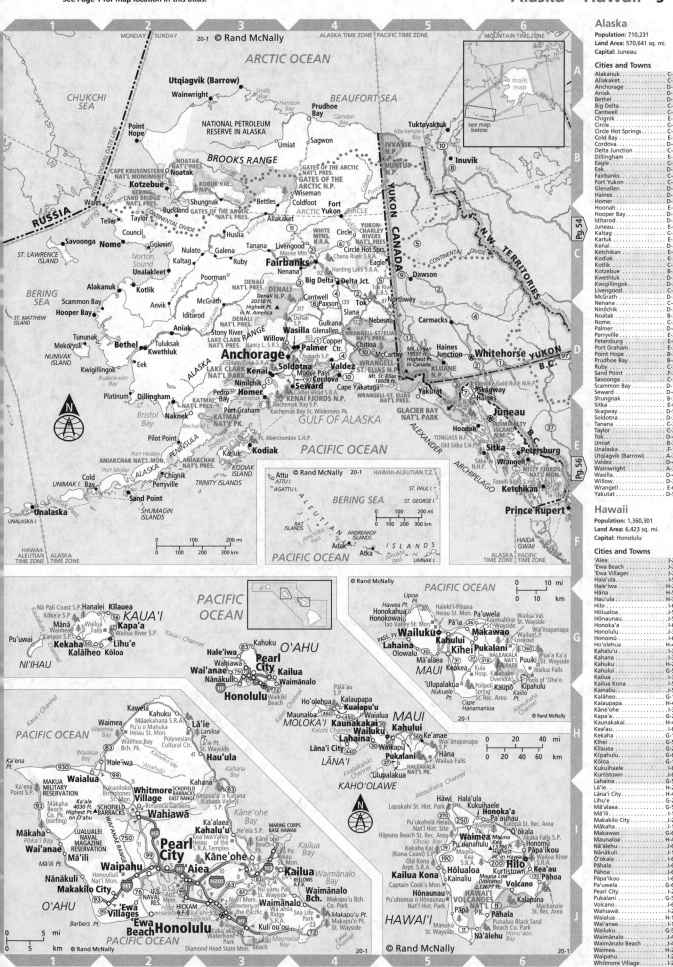

© Rand McNally

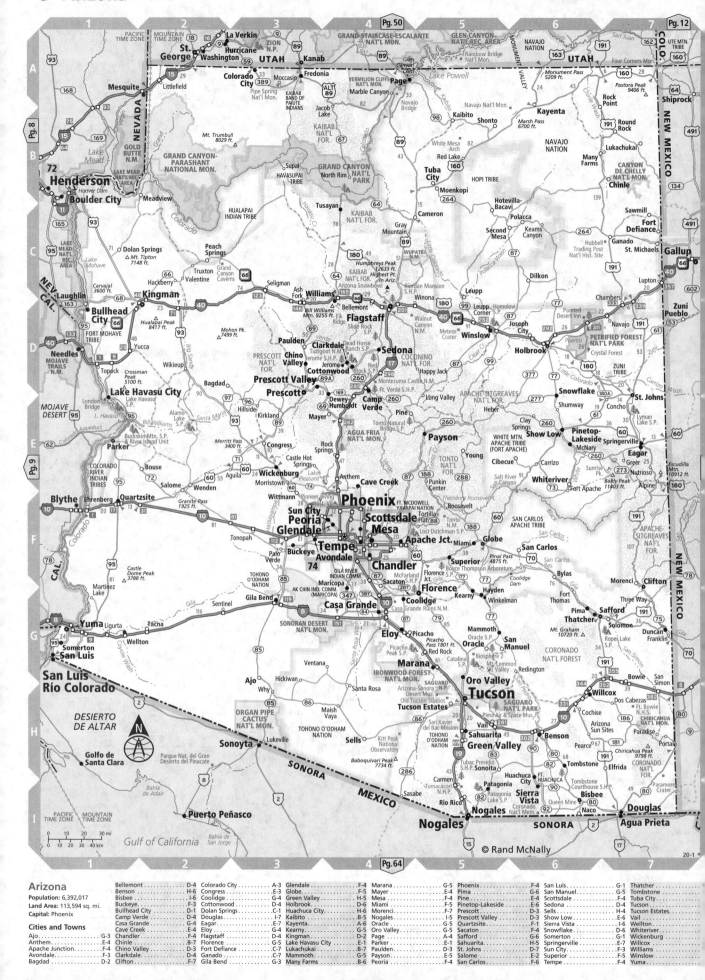

© Rand McNally

20-1

NOTE: Maps are not always in alphabetical order.
See Page 1 for map location in this atlas.

Arkansas 7

Pg. 20
Pg. 27
Pg. 42
Pg. 47
Pg. 23

NOTE: Maps are not always in alphabetical order.
See Page 1 for map location in this atlas.

California • Nevada 9

© Rand McNally

California
Population: 37,253,956
Land Area: 155,799 sq. mi.
Capital: Sacramento

Cities and Towns
Adelanto J-7
Alpine L-8
Alturas B-4
Anaheim J-7
Anderson D-2
Angels Camp E-3
Antioch F-3
Apple Valley J-7
Arcata C-1
Arroyo Grande I-4
Arvin I-6
Atascadero H-4
Atwater F-4
Auburn E-3
Avalon K-6
Avenal H-5
Bakersfield I-6
Barstow I-7
Bayview B-1
Beaumont J-8
Berkeley F-3
Bishop F-6
Blythe J-10
Borrego Springs ... K-8
Brawley K-9
Brentwood F-3
Bridgeport E-5
Buellton I-4
Calexico L-9
California City I-7
Calipatria K-9
Calistoga E-2
Cambria H-4
Camarillo I-5
Carlsbad K-7
Carmel-by-the-Sea .. G-4
Carpinteria I-5
Chico D-3
Chowchilla F-4
Chula Vista L-8
Clearlake Oaks E-2
Cloverdale E-2
Clovis G-5
Coalinga G-4
Colusa D-2
Corcoran H-5
Corning D-2
Corona J-7
Cotati E-2
Cottonwood C-3
Crescent City A-1
Delano I-5
Desert Hot Springs .. J-8
Dinuba G-5
Dixon E-3
Downieville D-4
Earlimart H-5
El Cajon L-8
El Centro K-9
Encinitas K-7
Escondido K-7
Eureka C-1
Exeter H-5
Fairfield E-3
Firebaugh G-4
Folsom E-3
Fort Bragg D-1
Fortuna C-1
Fowler G-5
Frazier Park I-6
Fremont F-3
Fresno G-4
Gilroy G-3
Glendale C-3
Grass Valley D-3
Greenfield G-4
Gridley D-3
Grover Beach I-4
Guadalupe I-4
Guerneville E-2
Gustine F-4
Hanford G-5
Healdsburg E-2
Hemet J-8
Hesperia J-7
Hollister G-4
Holtville K-9
Huron H-5
Imperial K-9
Independence G-6
Indio J-8
Ione E-3
Irvine J-7
Jackson E-4
Jamestown E-4
Kerman G-4
King City G-4
Kingsburg G-5
Lake Elsinore J-8
Lakeport E-2
Lancaster J-6
Lathrop F-4
Lemoore G-5
Lincoln D-3
Lindsay H-5
Livermore F-3
Livingston F-4
Lodi E-3
Loma Linda J-7
Lompoc I-4
Long Beach J-7
Los Angeles J-6
Los Banos G-4
Los Gatos F-3
Madera G-5
Manteca F-4
Mariposa F-5
Martinez F-3
Marysville D-3
McFarland H-5
Mendota G-4
Merced F-4
Milpitas F-3
Modesto F-4
Montecito I-5
Monterey G-3
Moorpark I-5
Morgan Hill G-4
Morro Bay H-4
Mount Shasta C-3
Napa E-2
National City L-8
Needles I-9
Nevada City D-3
Newman F-4
Newport Beach J-7
Novato E-2
Oakdale F-4
Oakland F-3
Oakley F-3
Oceanside K-7
Ojai I-5
Ontario J-7
Orland D-2
Oroville D-3
Oxnard I-5
Pacific Grove G-3
Palm Desert J-8
Palmdale J-6
Palo Alto F-3
Paradise D-3
Pasadena G-3
Paso Robles H-4
Patterson F-4
Perris J-8
Placerville E-3
Porterville H-5
Quincy D-4
Ramona K-8
Rancho Cordova ... E-3
Red Bluff C-2
Redding D-2
Redlands J-7
Redwood City F-3
Ridgecrest I-6
Rio Dell C-1
Rio Vista E-3
Rocklin D-3
Rosamond I-6
Roseville D-3
Sacramento E-3
Salinas G-4
San Andreas E-3
San Bernardino J-7
San Clemente J-7
San Diego L-8
San Francisco F-3
San Jacinto J-8
San Jose F-4
San Juan Capistrano . J-7
San Luis Obispo I-4
San Marcos K-7
Santa Ana J-7
Santa Barbara I-5
Santa Clarita J-6
Santa Cruz G-3
Santa Maria I-4
Santa Paula I-5
Santa Rosa E-2
Saratoga F-3
Seaside G-3
Sebastopol E-2
Selma G-5
Soledad G-4
Solvang I-4
Sonora E-3
South Lake Tahoe .. E-5
South San Francisco . F-3
Stockton F-4
Susanville C-4
Taft I-5
Tehachapi I-6
Temecula J-8
Thousand Oaks I-5
Tracy F-4
Truckee D-4
Tulare H-5
Turlock F-4
Twain Harte E-4
Twentynine Palms .. I-8
Ukiah D-2
Vacaville E-3
Vallejo E-3
Ventura I-5
Victorville J-7
Visalia H-5
Vista K-7
Wasco I-5
Watsonville G-4
Williams D-2
Willits D-2
Willows D-2
Winters E-3
Woodlake H-5
Woodland E-3
Yreka B-2
Yuba City D-3
Yucca Valley J-8

Nevada
Population: 2,700,551
Land Area: 109,781 sq. mi.
Capital: Carson City

Cities and Towns
Alamo F-9
Amargosa Valley ... G-8
Battle Mountain B-7
Beatty G-8
Boulder City H-9
Caliente F-10
Carlin B-8
Carson City D-5
Dayton D-5
Ely D-9
Eureka C-8
Fallon D-5
Fernley D-5
Gardnerville E-5
Hawthorne E-6
Henderson H-9
Indian Springs G-8
Jackpot A-9
Las Vegas H-9
Laughlin J-10
Lovelock C-6
McGill C-9
Mesquite G-9
Minden E-5
Overton G-9
Owyhee A-8
Pahrump H-8
Panaca F-10
Pioche F-10
Reno D-5
Schurz E-6
Searchlight H-9
Silver Springs D-5
Sparks D-5
Tonopah F-7
Verdi D-5
Virginia City D-5
Wadsworth D-5
Walker Lake E-6
Wells B-9
West Wendover B-10
Winnemucca B-7
Yerington E-5

NOTE: Maps are not always in alphabetical order.
See Page 1 for map location in this atlas.

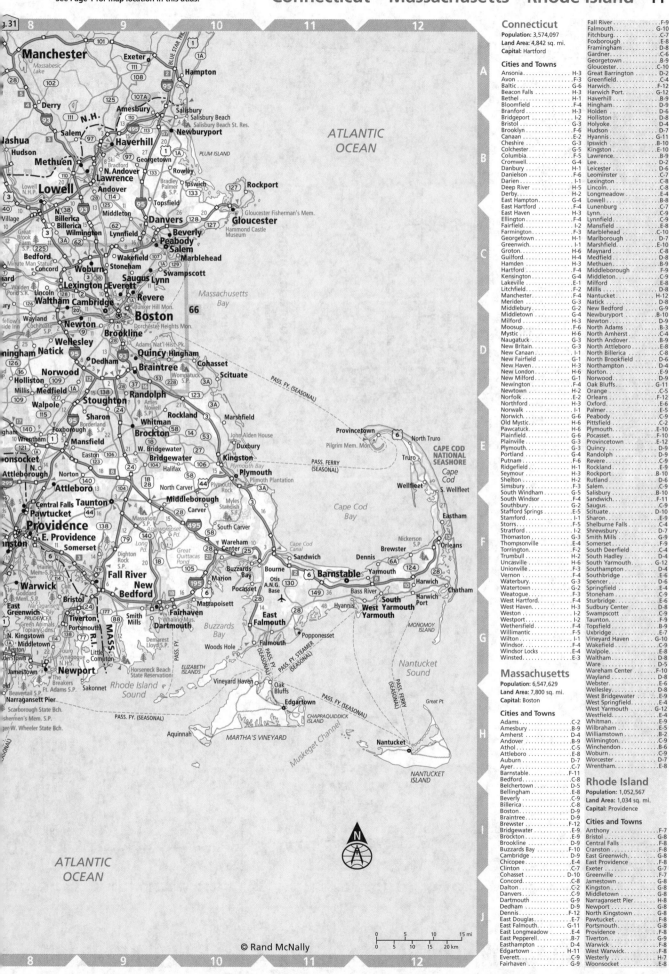

© Rand McNally

Connecticut
Population: 3,574,097
Land Area: 4,842 sq. mi.
Capital: Hartford

Cities and Towns

Ansonia	H-3
Avon	F-3
Baltic	G-6
Beacon Falls	H-3
Bethel	H-1
Bloomfield	F-4
Branford	H-3
Bridgeport	I-2
Bristol	G-3
Brooklyn	F-6
Canaan	C-2
Cheshire	G-3
Colchester	G-5
Columbia	F-5
Cromwell	G-4
Danbury	H-1
Danielson	F-6
Darien	I-1
Deep River	H-5
Derby	H-2
East Hampton	G-4
East Hartford	F-4
East Haven	H-3
Ellington	F-4
Fairfield	I-2
Farmington	F-3
Georgetown	H-1
Greenwich	I-1
Groton	H-6
Guilford	H-4
Hamden	H-3
Hartford	F-4
Kensington	G-4
Lakeville	E-1
Litchfield	F-2
Manchester	F-4
Meriden	G-3
Middlebury	G-2
Middletown	G-4
Milford	H-3
Moosup	F-6
Mystic	H-6
Naugatuck	G-3
New Britain	G-3
New Canaan	I-1
New Fairfield	G-1
New Haven	H-3
New London	H-6
New Milford	G-1
Newington	F-4
Newtown	H-2
Norfolk	E-2
Northford	H-3
Norwalk	I-1
Norwich	G-6
Old Mystic	H-6
Pawcatuck	H-6
Plainfield	G-6
Plainville	G-3
Plymouth	G-3
Portland	G-4
Putnam	F-6
Ridgefield	H-1
Seymour	H-2
Shelton	H-2
Simsbury	F-3
South Windham	G-5
South Windsor	F-4
Southbury	H-2
Stafford Springs	E-5
Stamford	I-1
Storrs	F-5
Stratford	I-2
Thomaston	G-3
Thompsonville	E-4
Torrington	F-2
Trumbull	H-2
Uncasville	H-6
Unionville	F-3
Vernon	F-5
Waterbury	G-3
Watertown	G-2
Weatogue	F-3
West Hartford	F-4
West Haven	H-3
Weston	I-1
Westport	I-2
Wethersfield	F-4
Willimantic	F-5
Wilton	I-1
Windsor	F-4
Windsor Locks	E-4
Winsted	E-3

Massachusetts
Population: 6,547,629
Land Area: 7,800 sq. mi.
Capital: Boston

Cities and Towns

Adams	C-2
Amesbury	B-9
Amherst	D-4
Andover	B-9
Athol	C-5
Attleboro	D-7
Auburn	D-7
Ayer	C-7
Barnstable	F-11
Bedford	C-8
Belchertown	D-5
Bellingham	E-8
Beverly	C-9
Billerica	C-8
Boston	D-9
Braintree	D-9
Brewster	F-12
Bridgewater	E-9
Brockton	E-9
Brookline	D-9
Buzzards Bay	F-10
Cambridge	D-9
Chicopee	E-4
Clinton	C-7
Cohasset	D-10
Concord	C-8
Dalton	C-2
Danvers	C-9
Dartmouth	G-9
Dedham	D-9
Dennis	F-12
East Douglas	E-7
East Falmouth	G-11
East Longmeadow	E-4
East Pepperell	B-7
Easthampton	D-4
Edgartown	H-11
Everett	C-9
Fairhaven	G-9

Fall River	F-9
Falmouth	G-10
Fitchburg	C-7
Foxborough	E-8
Framingham	D-8
Gardner	C-6
Georgetown	B-9
Gloucester	C-10
Great Barrington	D-2
Greenfield	C-4
Harwich	F-12
Harwich Port	G-12
Haverhill	B-9
Hingham	D-9
Holden	D-6
Holliston	D-8
Holyoke	D-4
Hudson	D-7
Hyannis	G-11
Ipswich	B-10
Kingston	E-10
Lawrence	B-9
Lee	D-2
Leicester	D-6
Leominster	C-7
Lexington	C-8
Lincoln	C-8
Longmeadow	E-4
Lowell	B-8
Lunenburg	C-7
Lynn	C-9
Lynnfield	C-9
Mansfield	E-8
Marblehead	C-10
Marlborough	D-7
Marshfield	E-10
Maynard	C-8
Medfield	D-8
Methuen	B-9
Middleborough	F-9
Middleton	C-9
Milford	E-8
Millis	D-8
Nantucket	H-12
Natick	D-8
New Bedford	G-9
Newburyport	B-10
Newton	D-9
North Adams	B-3
North Amherst	C-4
North Andover	B-9
North Attleboro	E-8
North Billerica	C-8
North Brookfield	D-6
Northampton	D-4
Norton	E-9
Norwood	D-9
Oak Bluffs	G-11
Orange	C-5
Orleans	F-12
Oxford	E-7
Palmer	E-5
Peabody	C-9
Pittsfield	C-2
Plymouth	E-10
Pocasset	F-10
Provincetown	E-12
Quincy	D-9
Randolph	D-9
Revere	C-9
Rockland	E-9
Rockport	B-10
Rutland	D-6
Salem	C-9
Salisbury	B-10
Sandwich	F-11
Saugus	C-9
Scituate	D-10
Sharon	E-9
Shelburne Falls	C-4
Shrewsbury	D-7
Smith Mills	G-9
Somerset	F-8
South Deerfield	C-4
South Hadley	D-4
South Yarmouth	G-12
Southampton	D-4
Southbridge	E-6
Spencer	D-6
Springfield	E-4
Stoneham	C-9
Sturbridge	E-6
Sudbury Center	D-8
Swampscott	C-9
Taunton	F-9
Topsfield	B-9
Uxbridge	E-7
Vineyard Haven	G-10
Wakefield	C-9
Walpole	E-8
Waltham	D-8
Ware	D-5
Wareham Center	F-10
Wayland	D-8
Webster	E-7
Wellesley	D-8
West Bridgewater	E-9
West Springfield	E-4
West Yarmouth	G-12
Westfield	E-4
Whitman	E-9
Wilbraham	E-5
Williamstown	B-2
Wilmington	C-9
Winchendon	B-6
Woburn	C-9
Worcester	D-7
Wrentham	E-8

Rhode Island
Population: 1,052,567
Land Area: 1,034 sq. mi.
Capital: Providence

Cities and Towns

Anthony	F-7
Bristol	G-8
Central Falls	F-8
Cranston	F-8
East Greenwich	G-8
East Providence	F-8
Exeter	G-7
Greenville	F-7
Jamestown	G-8
Kingston	G-8
Middletown	G-8
Narragansett Pier	H-8
Newport	G-8
North Kingstown	G-8
Pawtucket	F-8
Portsmouth	G-8
Providence	F-8
Tiverton	G-9
Warwick	F-8
West Warwick	F-8
Westerly	H-7
Woonsocket	E-8

12 Colorado

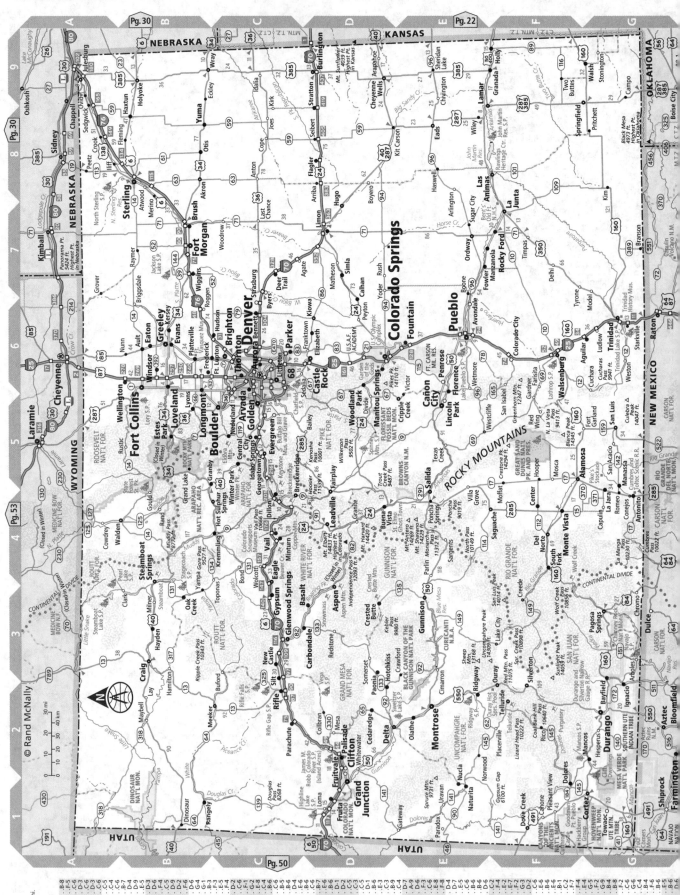

Colorado

Population: 5,029,196
Land Area: 103,642 sq. mi.
Capital: Denver

Cities and Towns

Akron B-8
Alamosa F-5
Arvada C-6
Aurora C-6
Aspen D-3
Basalt D-3
Bennett C-6
Boulder C-5
Breckenridge C-5
Brighton C-6
Brush B-7
Buena Vista D-4
Burlington C-9
Canon City E-5
Carbondale D-3
Castle Rock C-6
Center F-4
Central City C-5
Cheyenne Wells C-9
Clifton D-2
Colorado City E-6
Colorado Springs D-6
Conejos F-5
Cortez F-1
Craig B-3
Creede E-4
Cripple Creek D-5
Del Norte F-4
Delta E-2
Denver C-6
Dove Creek F-1
Durango F-2
Eads D-8
Eagle D-4
Eaton B-6
Elizabeth C-6
Englewood C-6
Estes Park B-5
Evans B-6
Fairplay D-5
Florence E-5
Fort Collins B-6
Fort Lupton C-6
Fort Morgan B-7
Fountain D-6
Fowler E-6
Frederick C-6
Fruita D-1
Fruitvale D-2
Georgetown C-5
Glenwood Springs D-3
Golden C-6
Granby C-5
Grand Junction D-1
Greeley B-6
Gunnison E-3
Gypsum D-3
Haxtun A-8
Holyoke A-9
Hot Sulphur Springs C-5
Hugo D-7
Idaho Springs C-5
Julesburg A-9
Kiowa C-6
Kit Carson D-8
Lakewood C-6
Lamar E-8
Las Animas E-7
Leadville D-4
Limon D-7
Littleton C-6
Longmont B-6
Louisville C-5
Loveland B-6
Manitou Springs D-6
Meeker C-2
Monte Vista F-4
Montrose E-2
Ordway E-7
Ouray E-2
Pagosa Springs F-3
Palisade D-2
Parker C-6
Penrose E-5
Petroville E-2
Pueblo E-6
Rangely C-1
Rifle D-3
Rocky Ford E-7
Saguache E-4
Salida E-4
San Luis F-5
Silverton E-2
Springfield F-8
Steamboat Springs B-4
Sterling B-8
Telluride E-2
Thornton C-6
Trinidad F-6
Vail D-4
Walden B-4
Walsenburg F-6
Westcliffe E-5
Wellington B-6
Wray B-9

© Rand McNally

Florida

Population: 18,801,310
Land Area: 53,625 sq. mi.
Capital: Tallahassee

Cities and Towns

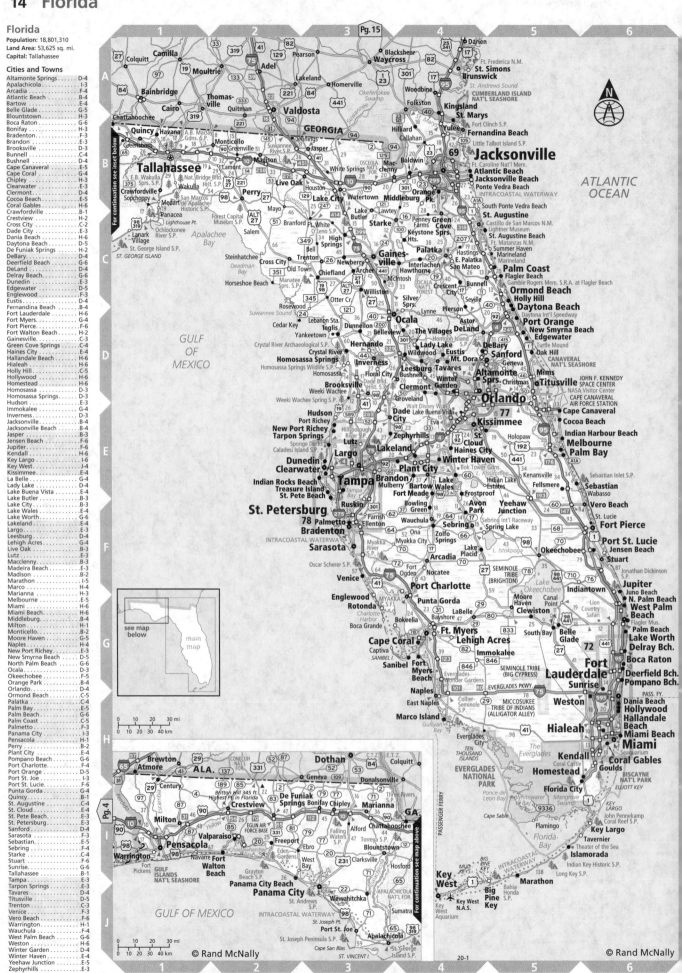

© Rand McNally

NOTE: Maps are not always in alphabetical order.
See Page 1 for map location in this atlas.

Georgia 15

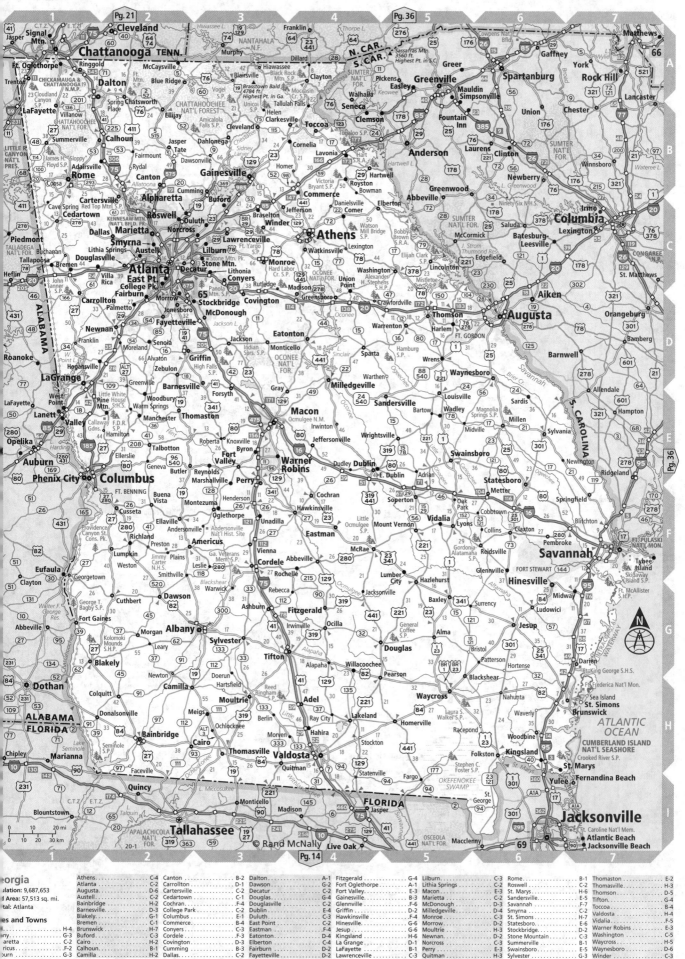

© Rand McNally

Idaho

Population: 1,567,582
Land Area: 82,643 sq. mi.
Capital: Boise

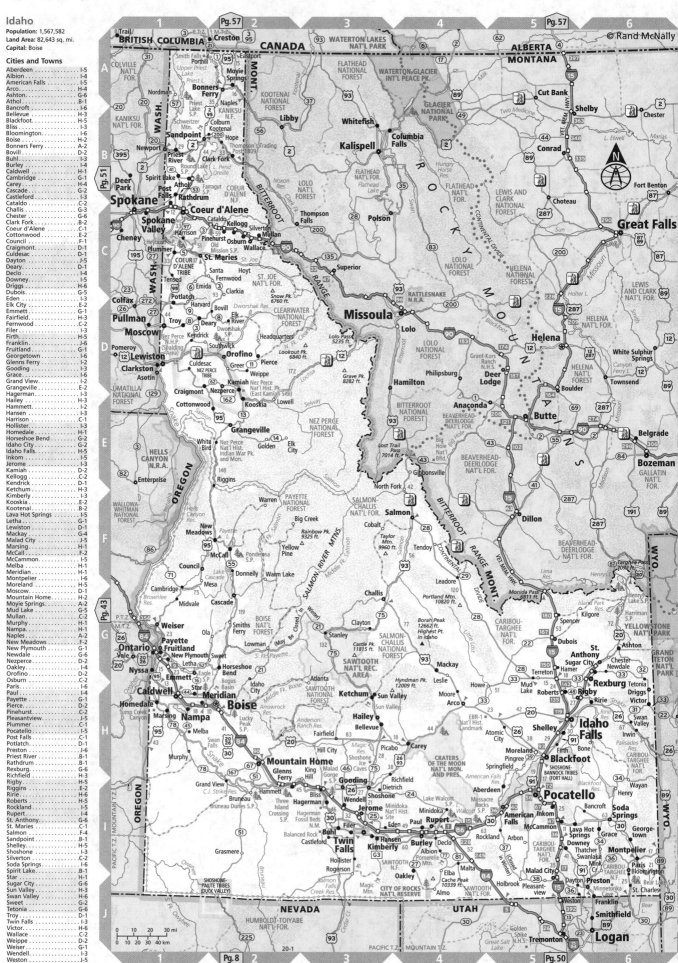

© Rand McNally

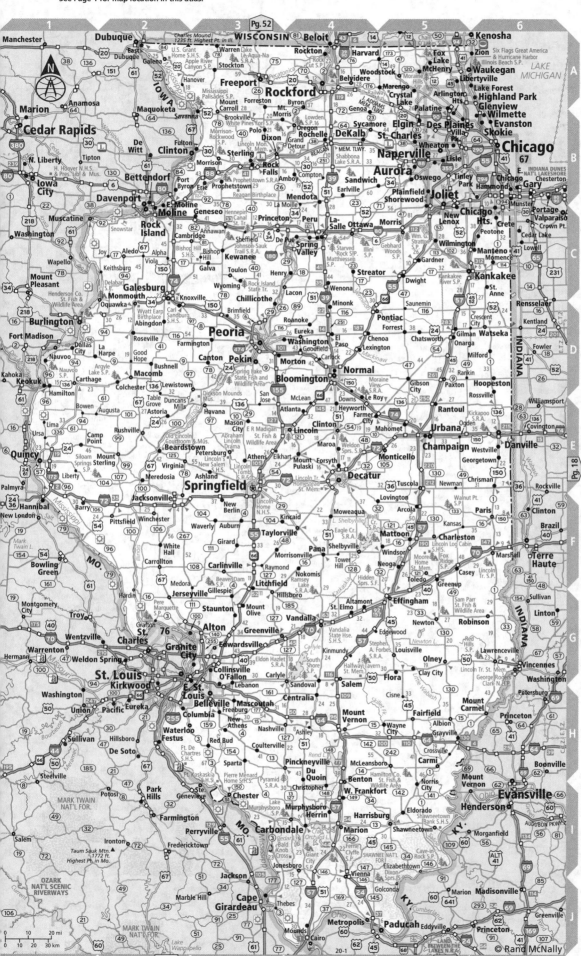

Illinois
Population: 12,830,632
Land Area: 55,519 sq. mi.
Capital: Springfield

Indiana

Population: 6,483,802
Land Area: 35,826 sq. mi.
Capital: Indianapolis

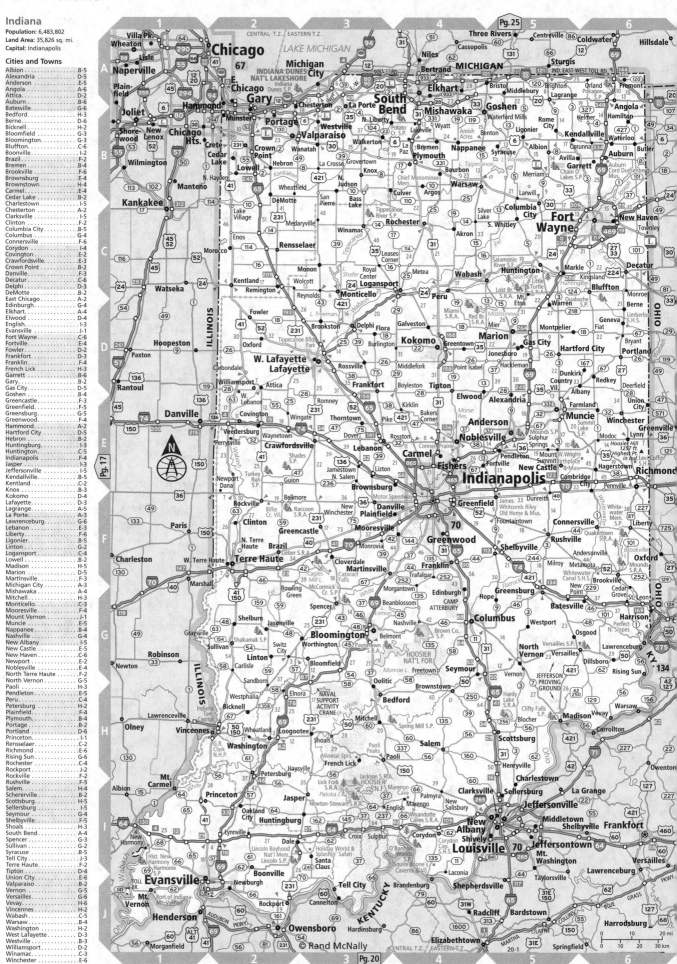

© Rand McNally

Pg. 25
Pg. 17
Pg. 20

NOTE: Maps are not always in alphabetical order.
See Page 1 for map location in this atlas.

Iowa 19

© Rand McNally

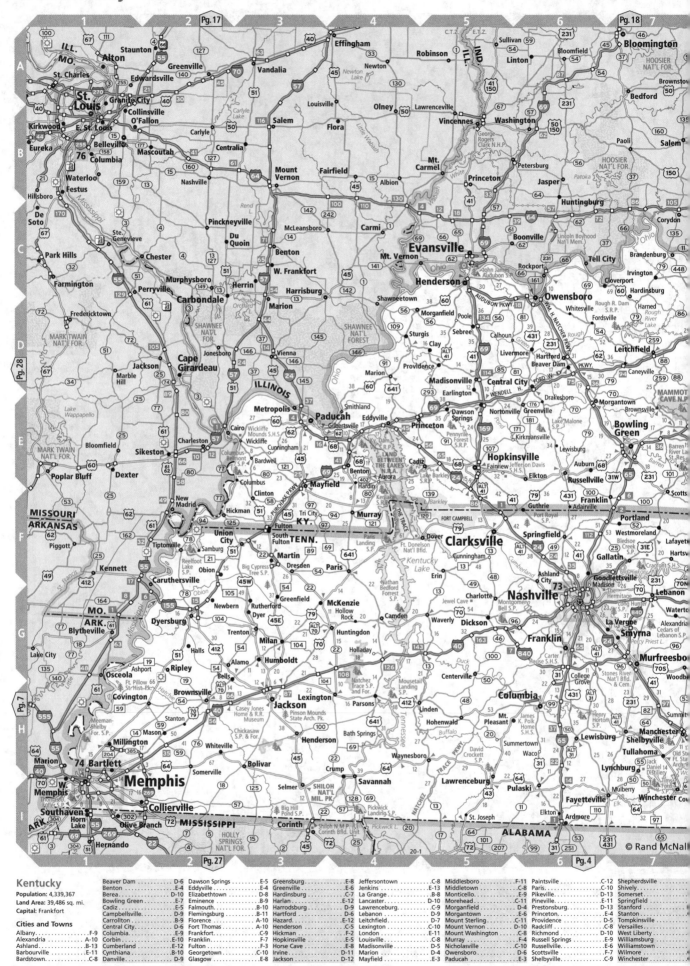

© Rand McNally

NOTE: Maps are not always in alphabetical order.
See Page 1 for map location in this atlas.

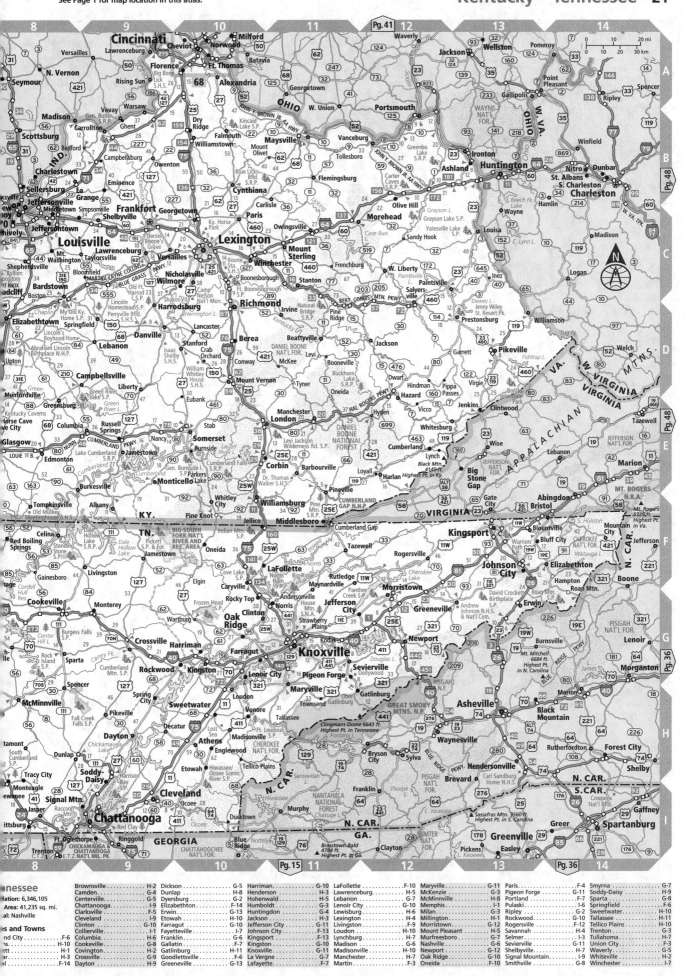

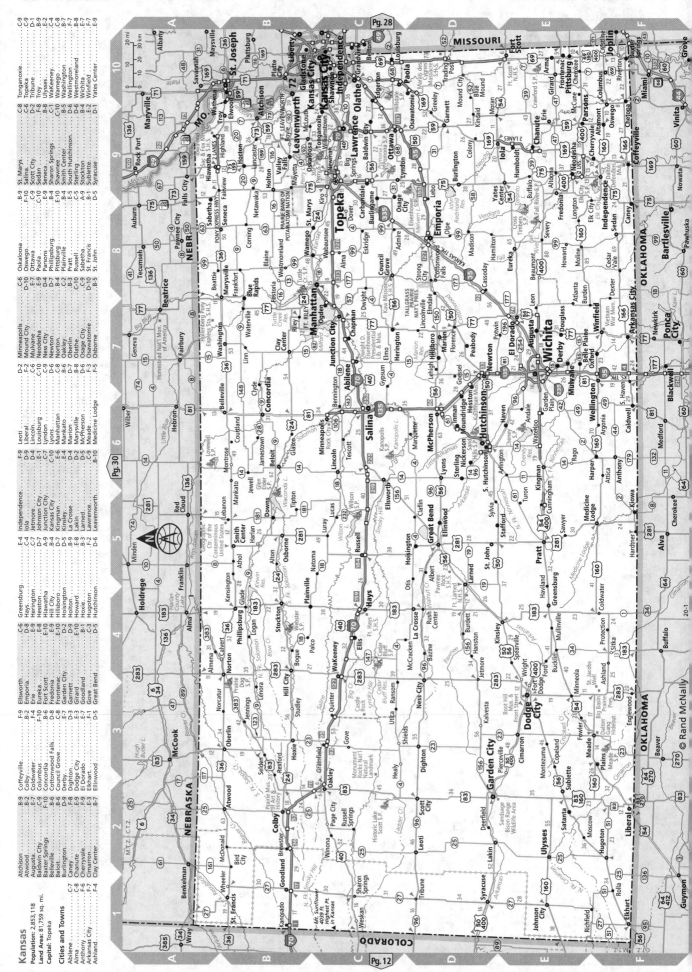

Kansas

Population: 2,853,118
Land Area: 81,759 sq. mi.
Capital: Topeka

Cities and Towns

NOTE: Maps are not always in alphabetical order.
See Page 1 for map location in this atlas.

Louisiana 23

© Rand McNally

Population: 4,533,372
Land Area: 43,204 sq. mi.
Capital: Baton Rouge

Cities and Towns

Pg. 27
Pg. 47

Maine

Population: 1,328,361
Land Area: 30,843 sq. mi.
Capital: Augusta

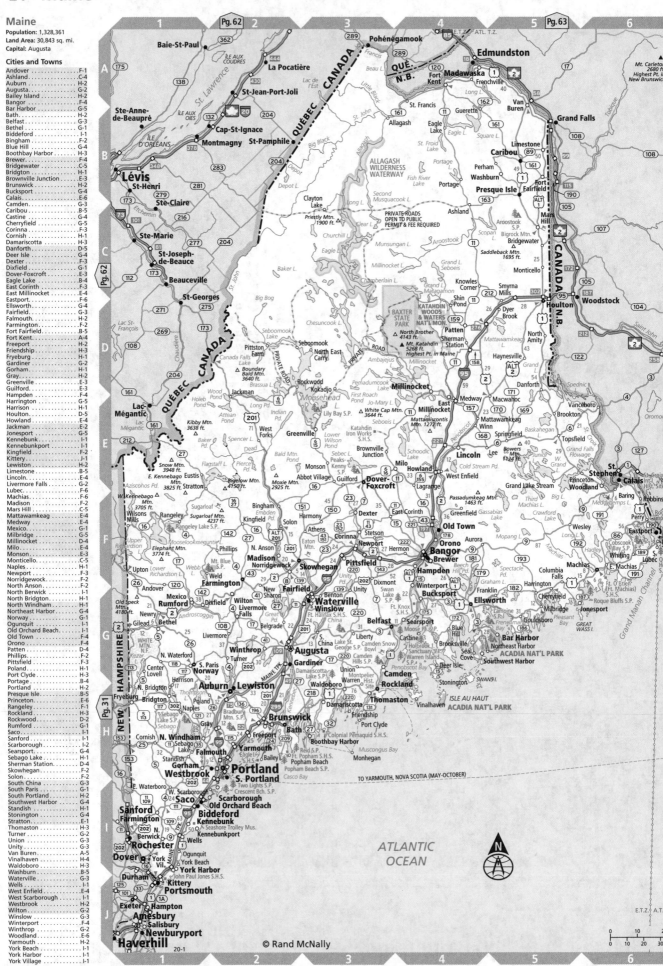

© Rand McNally

20-1

NOTE: Maps are not always in alphabetical order.
See Page 1 for map location in this atlas.

© Rand McNally

© Rand McNally

Michigan

Population: 9,883,640
Land Area: 56,539 sq. mi.
Capital: Lansing

Minnesota
Population: 5,303,925
Land Area: 79,627 sq. mi.
Capital: St. Paul

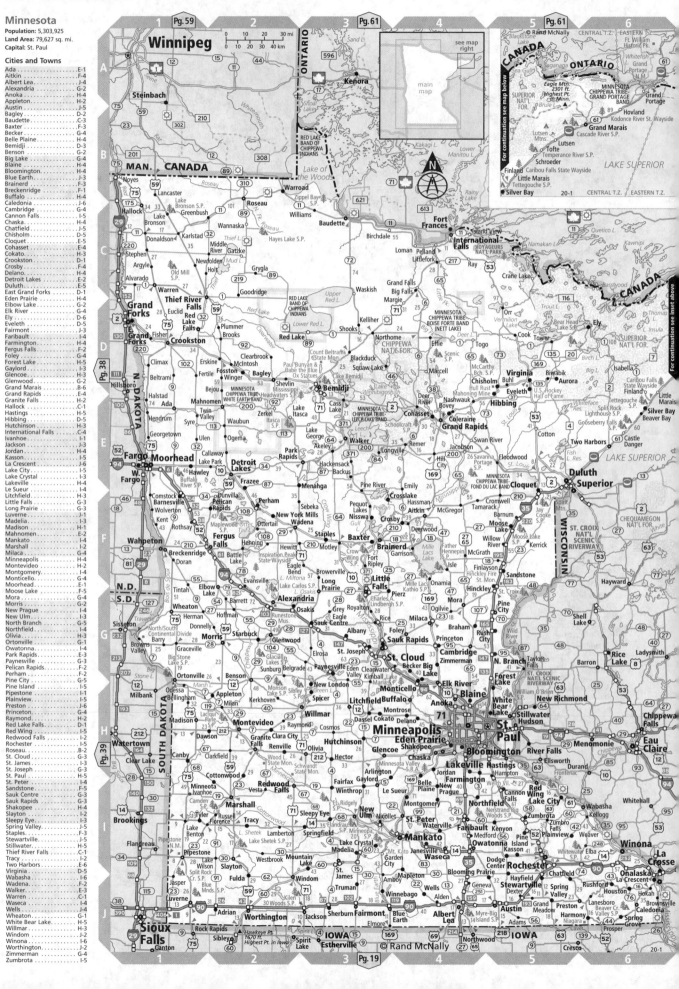

© Rand McNally

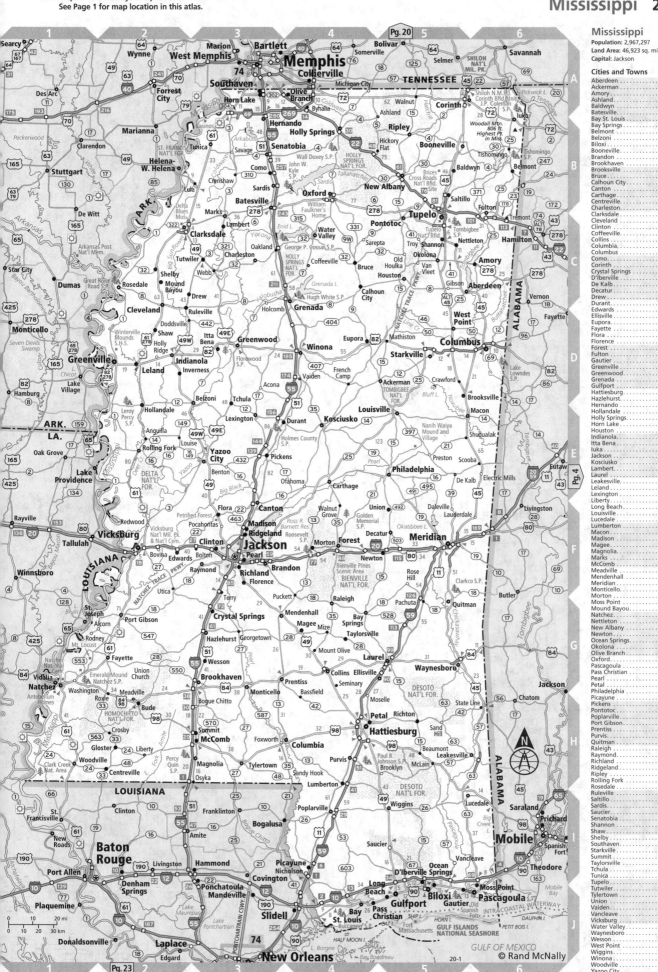

Pg. 17 Pg. 20 Pg. 30 Pg. 22 Pg. 42 Pg. 19

© Rand McNally

Missouri
Population: 5,988,927
Land Area: 68,741 sq. mi.
Capital: Jefferson City

ARKANSAS KANSAS OKLAHOMA IOWA ILL. KY. TENN. NEB.

Mississippi Missouri Ohio

OZARK NAT'L. SCENIC RIVERWAYS MARK TWAIN NAT'L. FOR. SHAWNEE NAT'L. FOR.

NOTE: Maps are not always in alphabetical order.
See Page 1 for map location in this atlas.

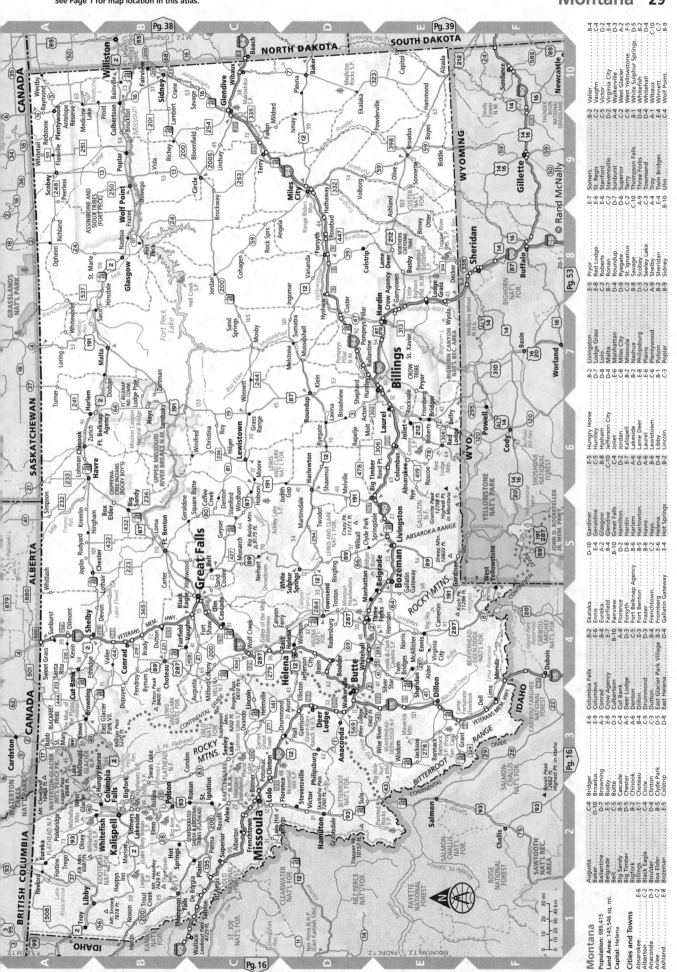

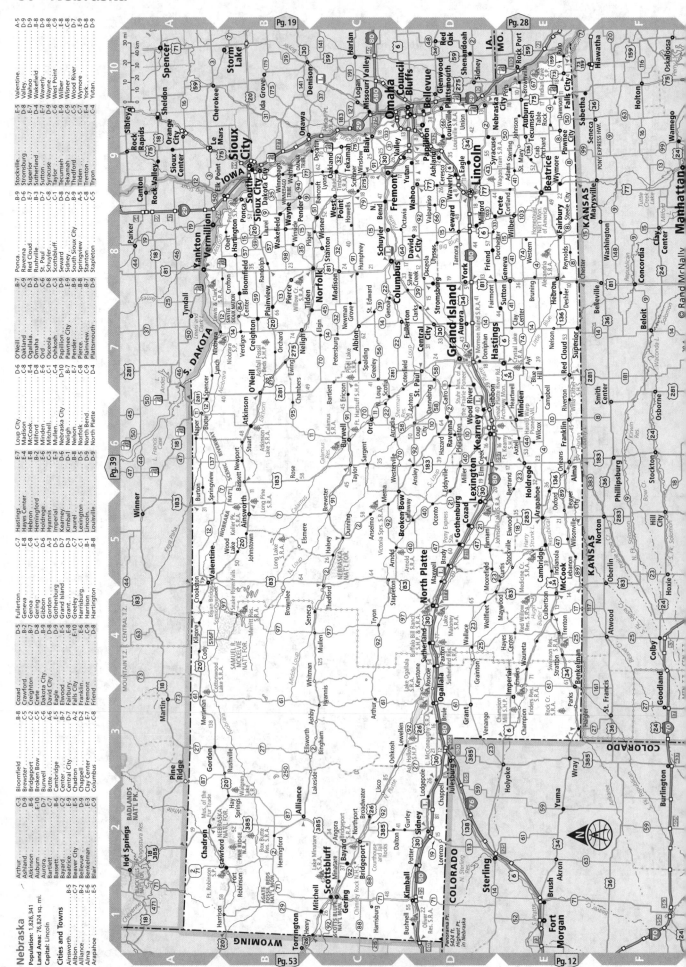

NOTE: Maps are not always in alphabetical order.
See Page 1 for map location in this atlas.

New Hampshire • Vermont 31

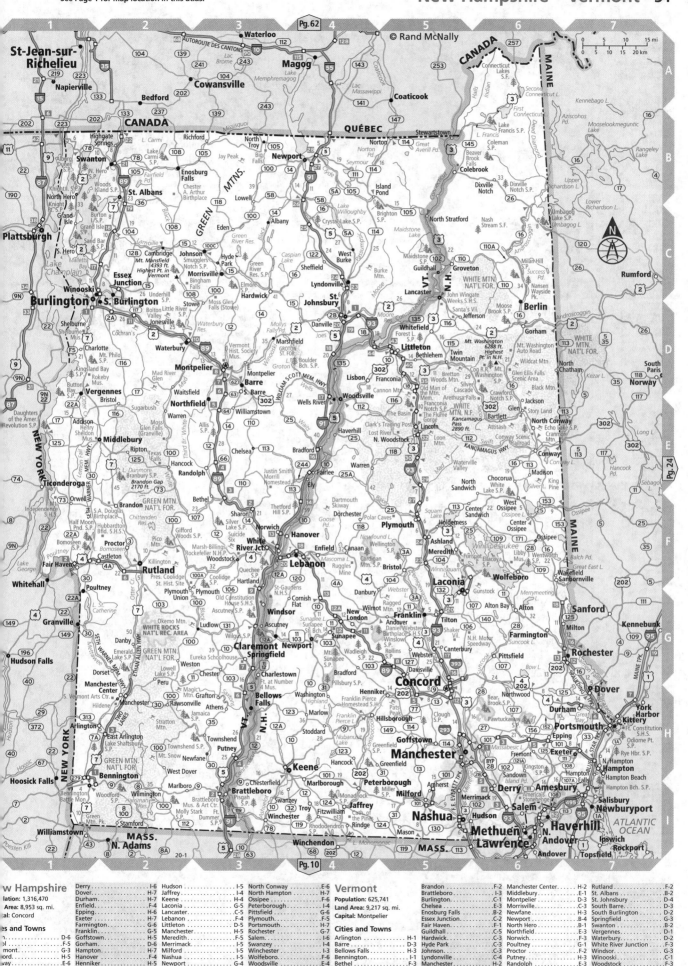

© Rand McNally

New Jersey
Population: 8,791,894
Land Area: 7,354 sq. mi.
Capital: Trenton

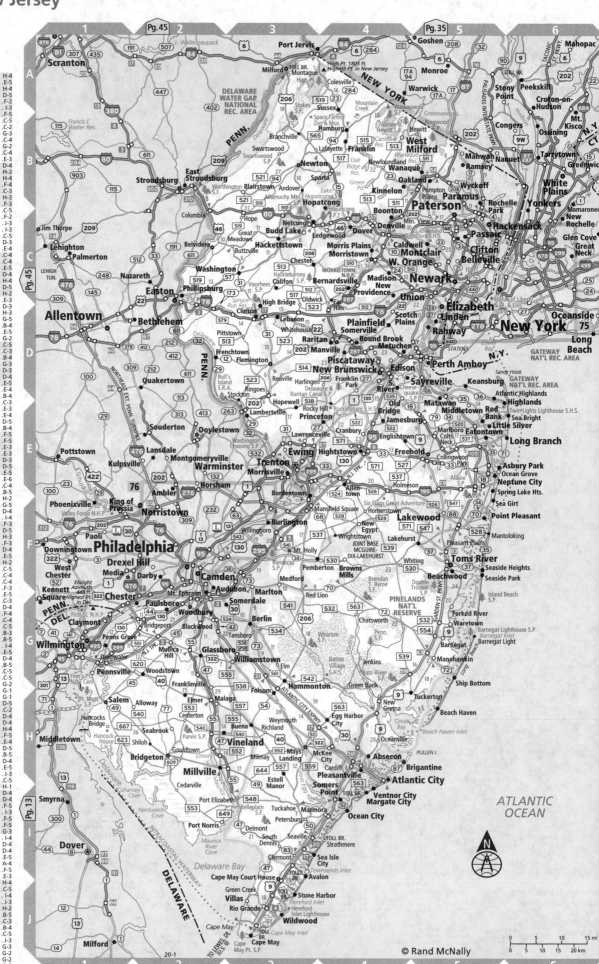

© Rand McNally

NOTE: Maps are not always in alphabetical order.
See Page 1 for map location in this atlas.

© Rand McNally

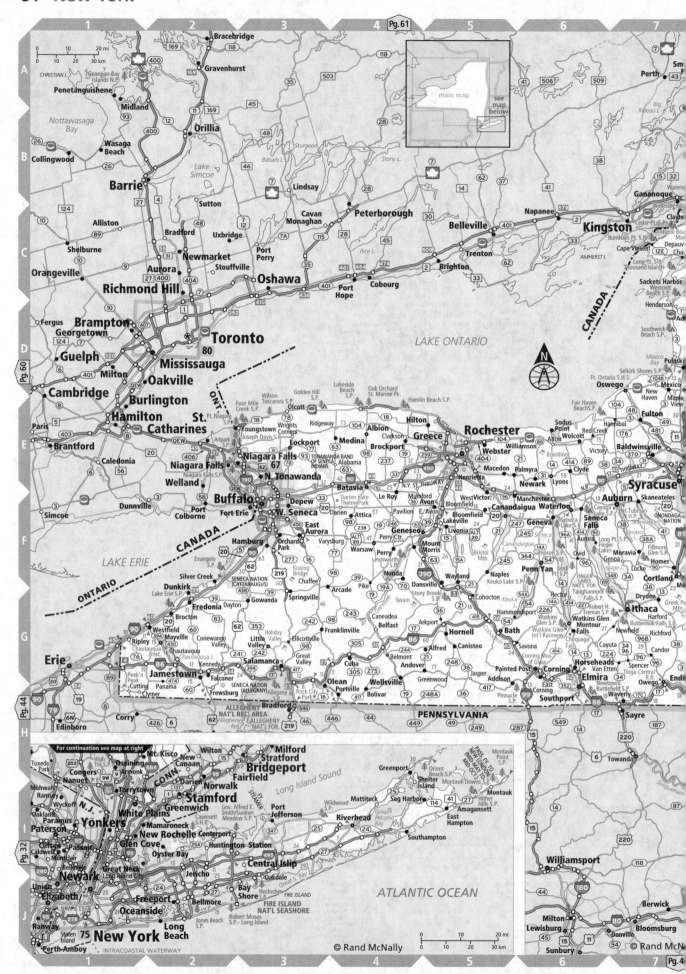

© Rand McNally

NOTE: Maps are not always in alphabetical order.
See Page 1 for map location in this atlas.

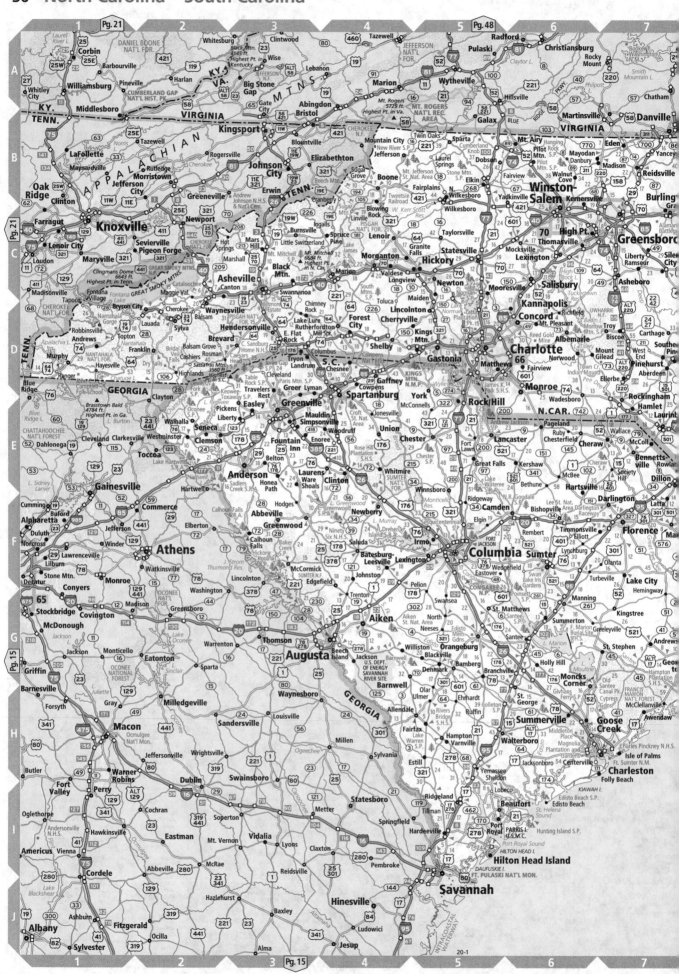

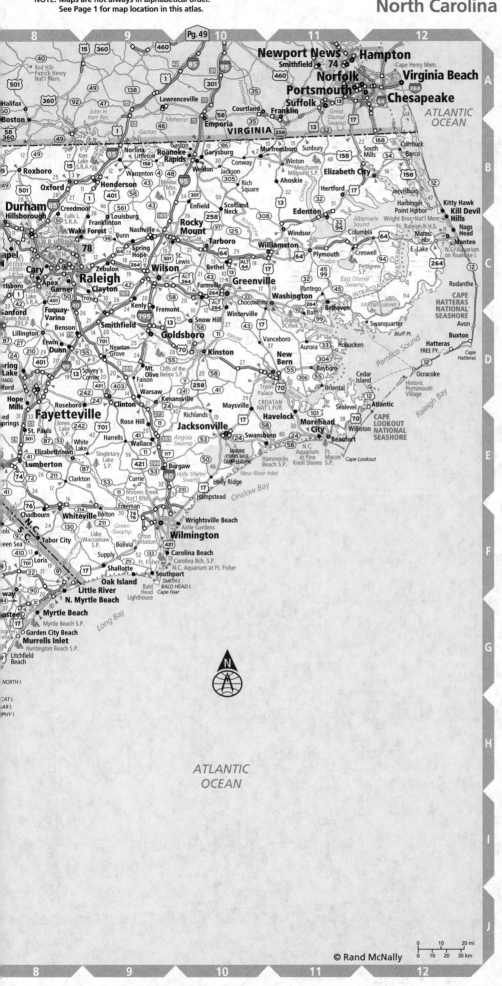

NOTE: Maps are not always in alphabetical order.
See Page 1 for map location in this atlas.

© Rand McNally

ATLANTIC OCEAN

North Carolina
Population: 9,535,483
Land Area: 48,618 sq. mi.
Capital: Raleigh

South Carolina
Population: 4,625,364
Land Area: 30,061 sq. mi.
Capital: Columbia

North Dakota

Population: 672,591
Land Area: 69,000 sq. mi.
Capital: Bismarck

© Rand McNally

Pg. 26
Pg. 29
Pg. 58
Pg. 59

NOTE: Maps are not always in alphabetical order.
See Page 1 for map location in this atlas.

South Dakota 39

Pg. 44
Pg. 60
Pg. 25
Pg. 18
Pg. 25

NOTE: Maps are not always in alphabetical order.
See Page 1 for map location in this atlas.

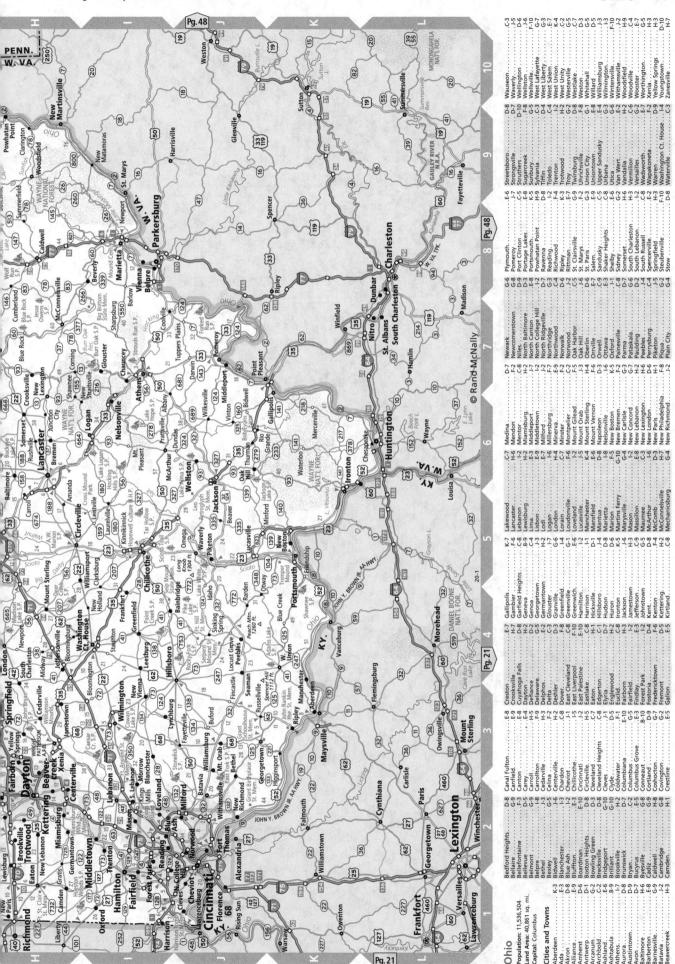

© Rand McNally

Oklahoma

Population: 3,751,351
Land Area: 68,595 sq. mi.
Capital: Oklahoma City

Cities and Towns

Pg. 28 · Pg. 7 · Pg. 22 · Pg. 12 · Pg. 33 · Pg. 46

© Rand McNally

NOTE: Maps are not always in alphabetical order.
See Page 1 for map location in this atlas.

© Rand McNally

Population: 3,831,074
Land Area: 95,988 sq. mi.
Capital: Salem

PACIFIC OCEAN

IDAHO

WASHINGTON

NEVADA

CALIFORNIA

Pg. 16
Pg. 8

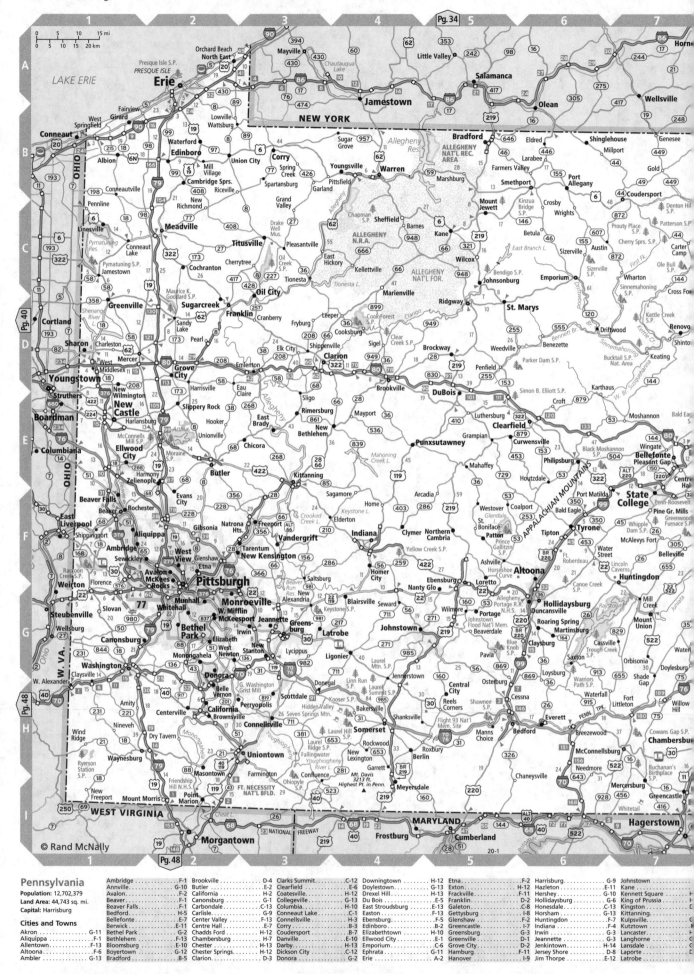

Pg. 34

Pg. 40

Pg. 48

© Rand McNally

Pennsylvania

Population: 12,702,379
Land Area: 44,743 sq. mi.
Capital: Harrisburg

Cities and Towns

NOTE: Maps are not always in alphabetical order.
See Page 1 for map location in this atlas.

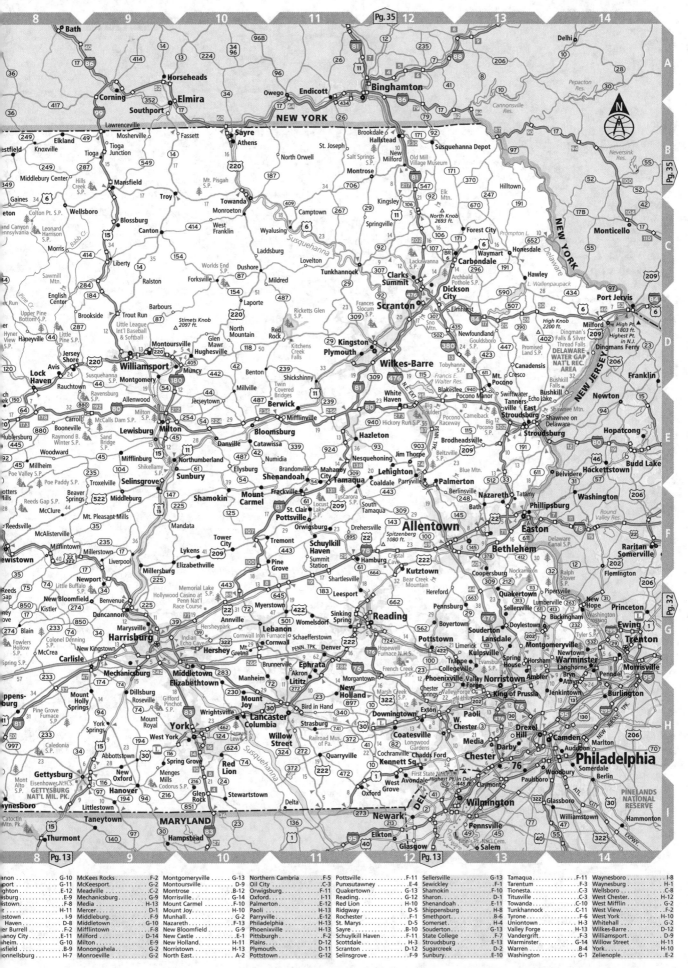

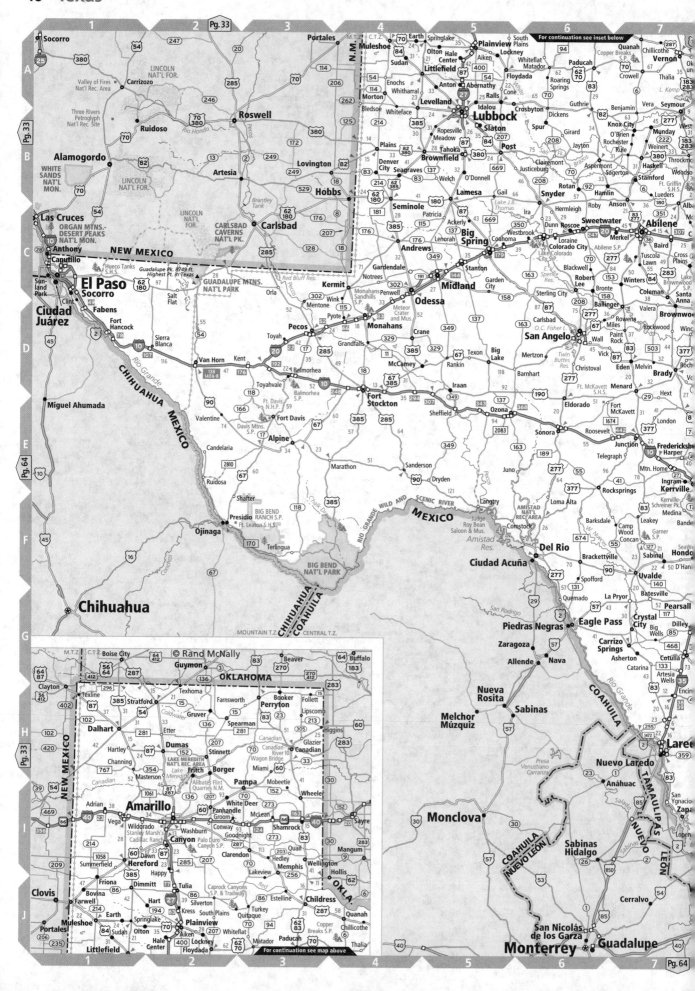

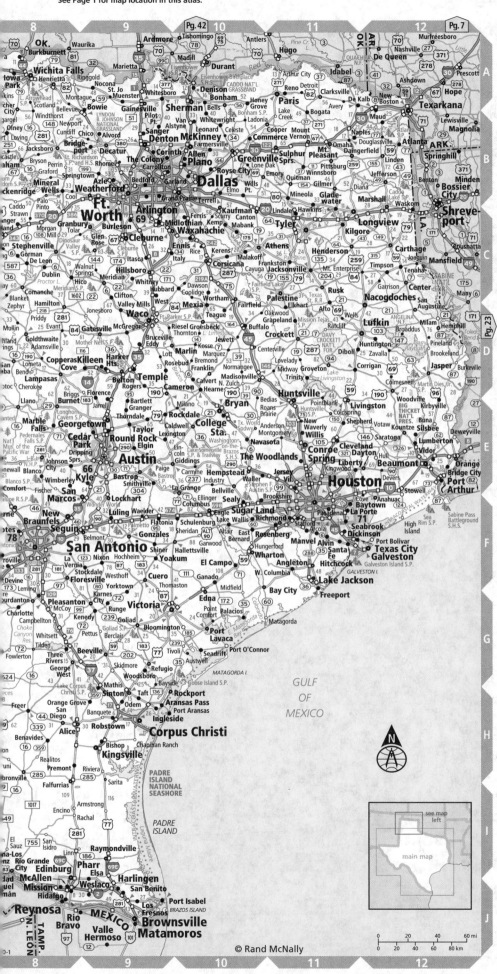

NOTE: Maps are not always in alphabetical order.
See Page 1 for map location in this atlas.

Texas

Population: 25,145,561
Land Area: 261,231 sq. mi.
Capital: Austin

Cities and Towns

Pg. 42
Pg. 7
Pg. 23

GULF OF MEXICO

PADRE ISLAND NATIONAL SEASHORE

PADRE ISLAND

see map left

main map

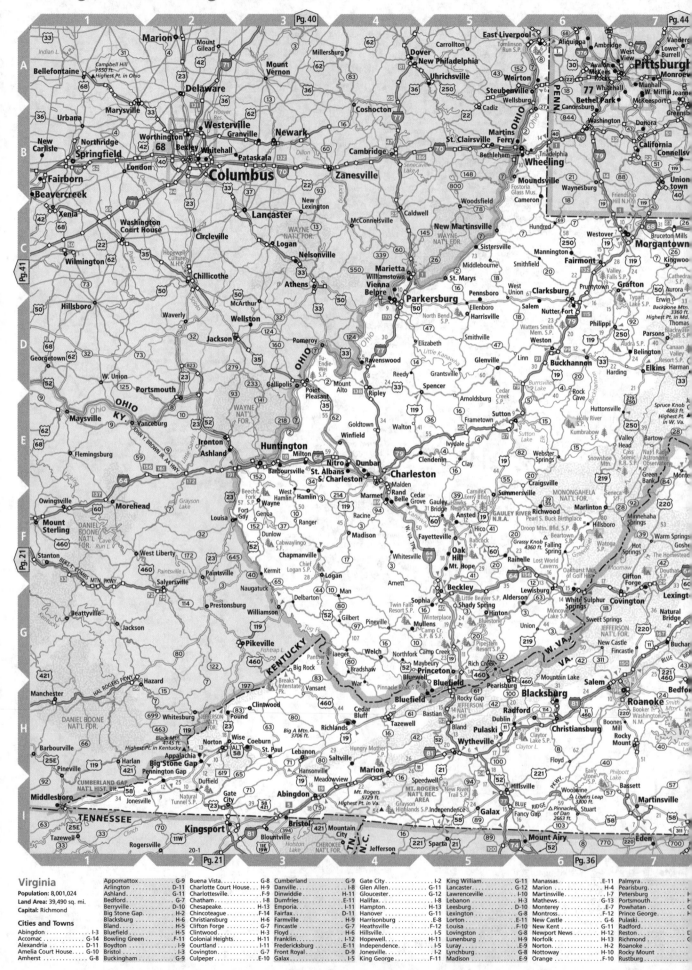

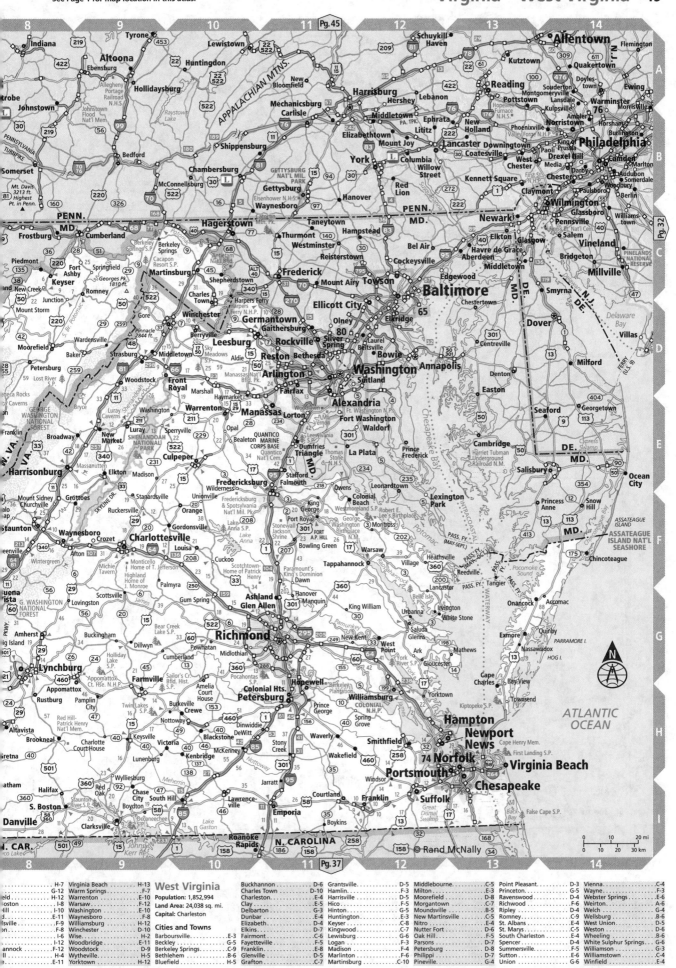

© Rand McNally

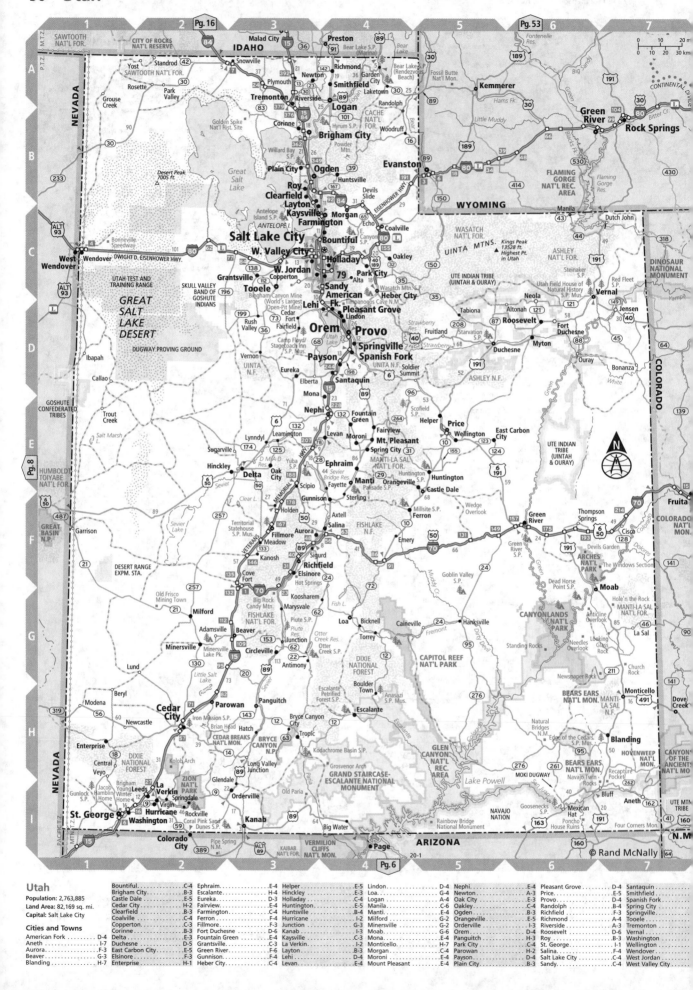

Pg. 16
Pg. 53
Pg. 8
Pg. 6

Utah

Population: 2,763,885
Land Area: 82,169 sq. mi.
Capital: Salt Lake City

Cities and Towns

NOTE: Maps are not always in alphabetical order.
See Page 1 for map location in this atlas.

Washington 51

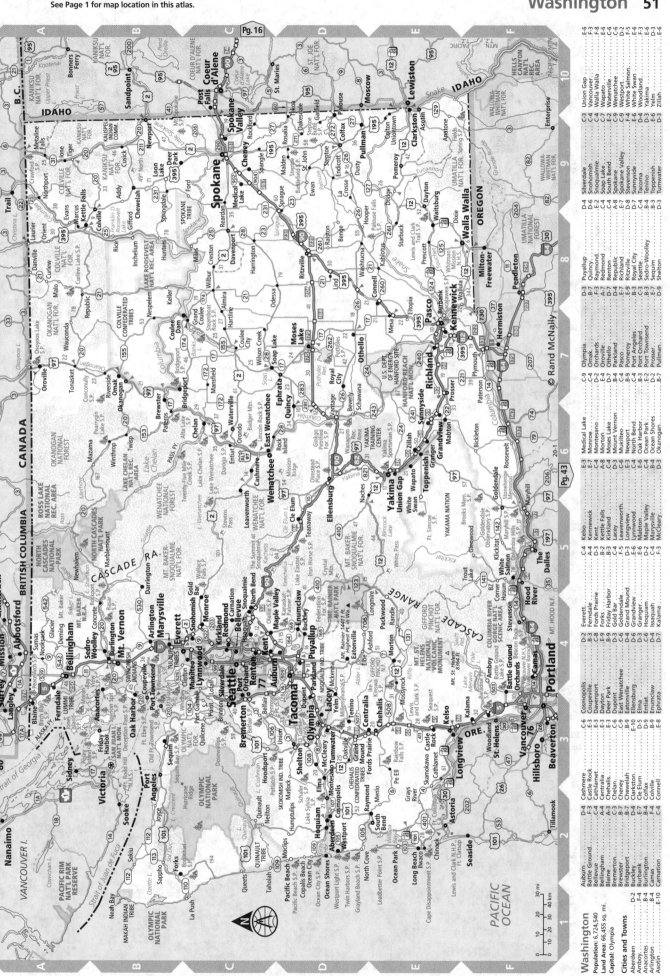

© Rand McNally

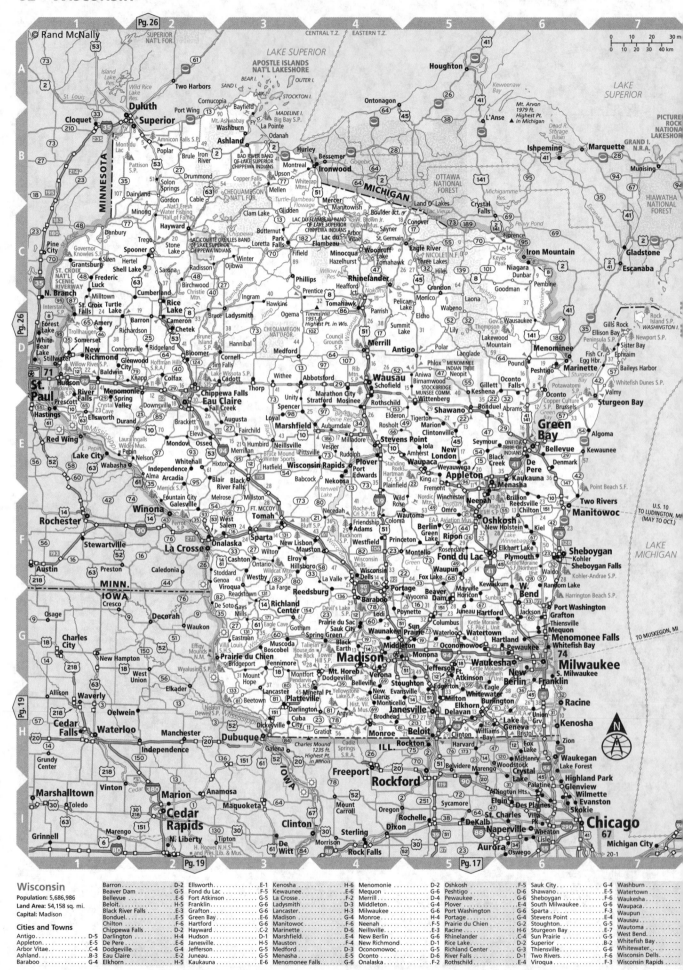

NOTE: Maps are not always in alphabetical order.
See Page 1 for map location in this atlas.

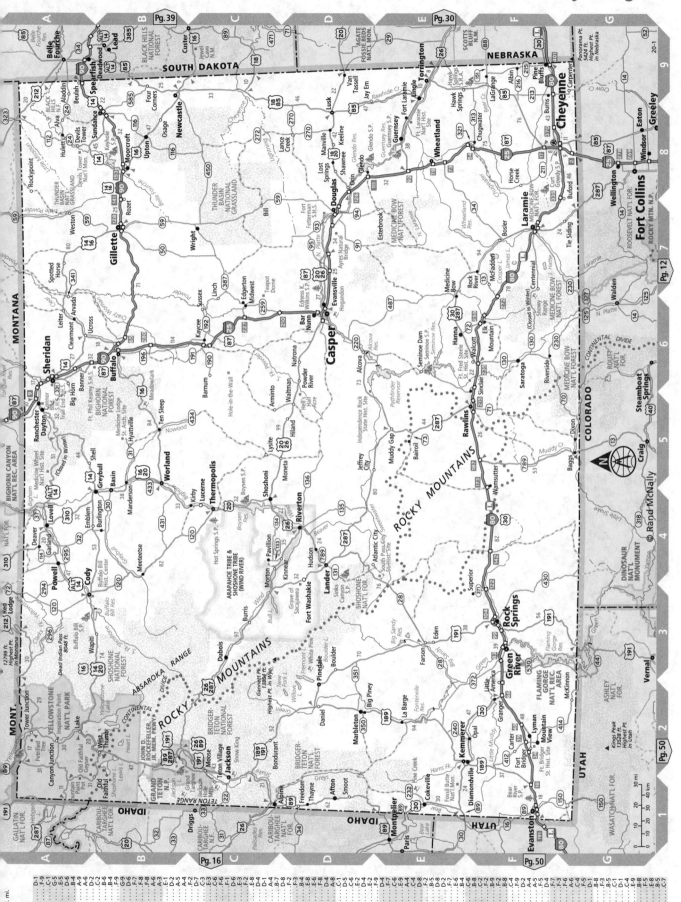

Land Area: 97,093 sq. mi.
Capital: Cheyenne

Pg. 39

Pg. 30

Pg. 12

Pg. 16

Pg. 50

© Rand McNally

Pg. 2

© Rand McNally

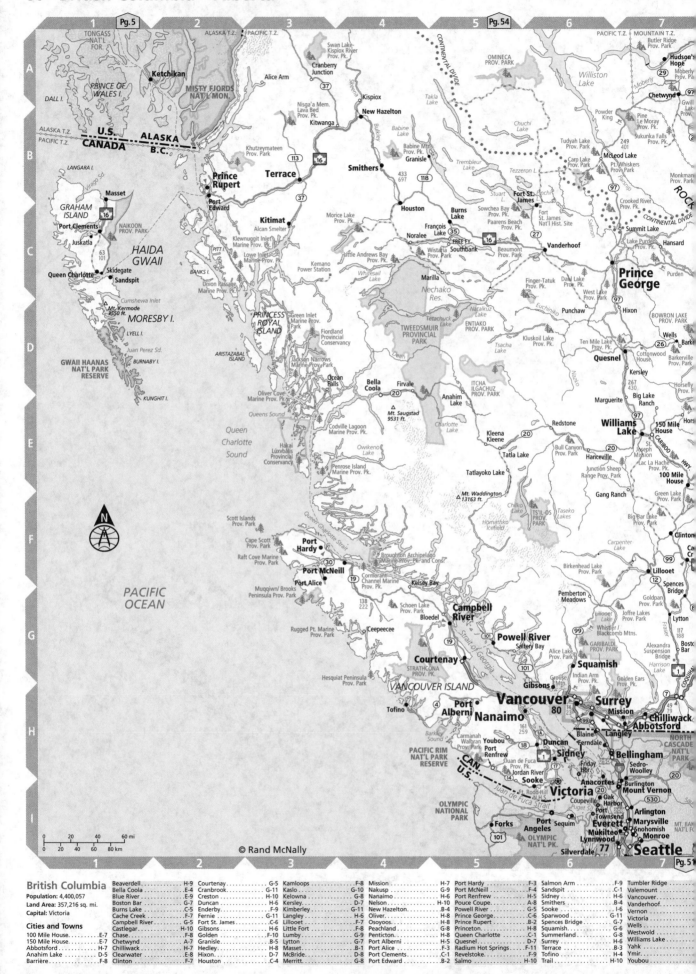

© Rand McNally

NOTE: Maps are not always in alphabetical order.
See Page 1 for map location in this atlas.

British Columbia • Alberta   57

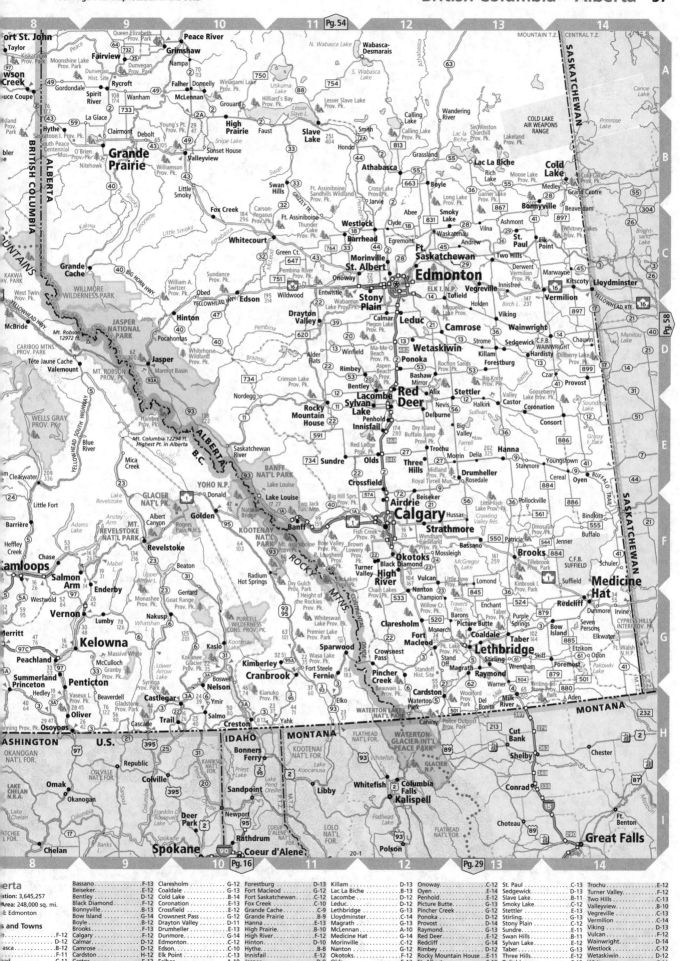

© Rand McNally

NOTE: Maps are not always in alphabetical order.
See Page 1 for map location in this atlas.

Saskatchewan • Manitoba 59

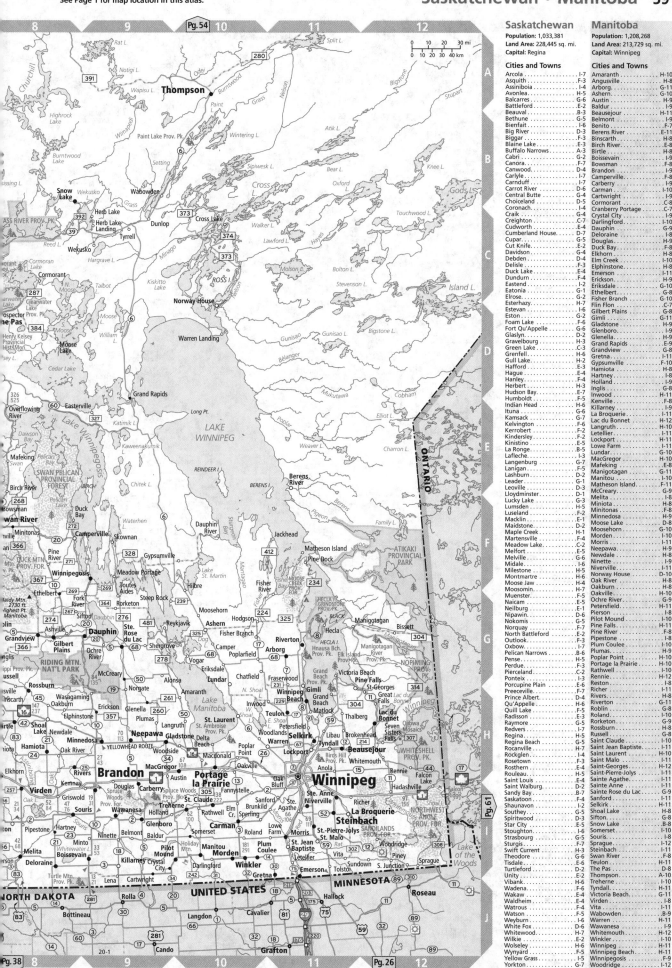

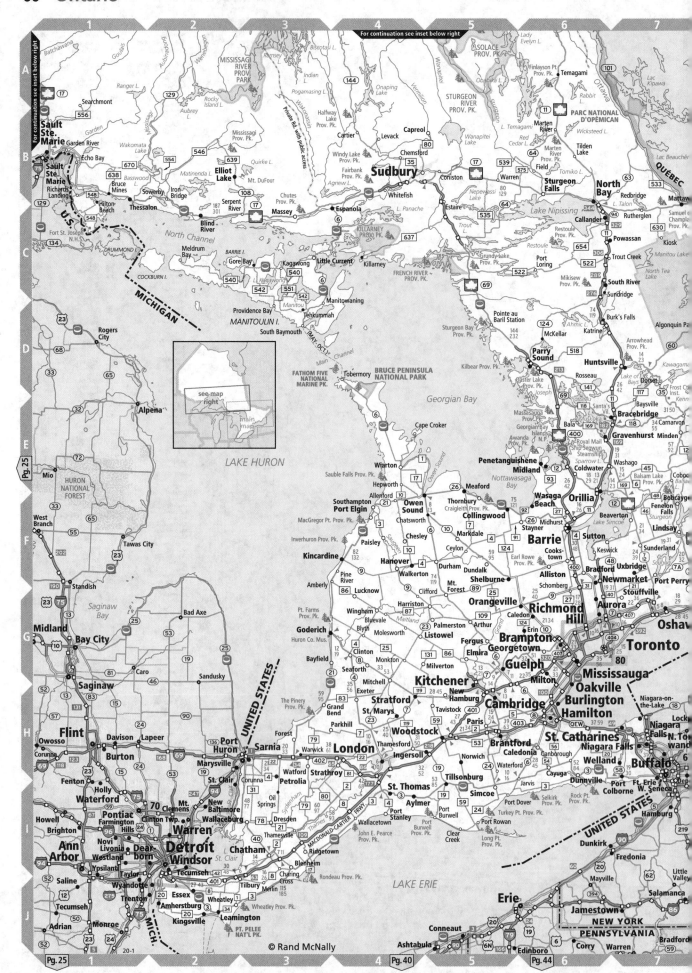

For continuation see inset below right

© Rand McNally

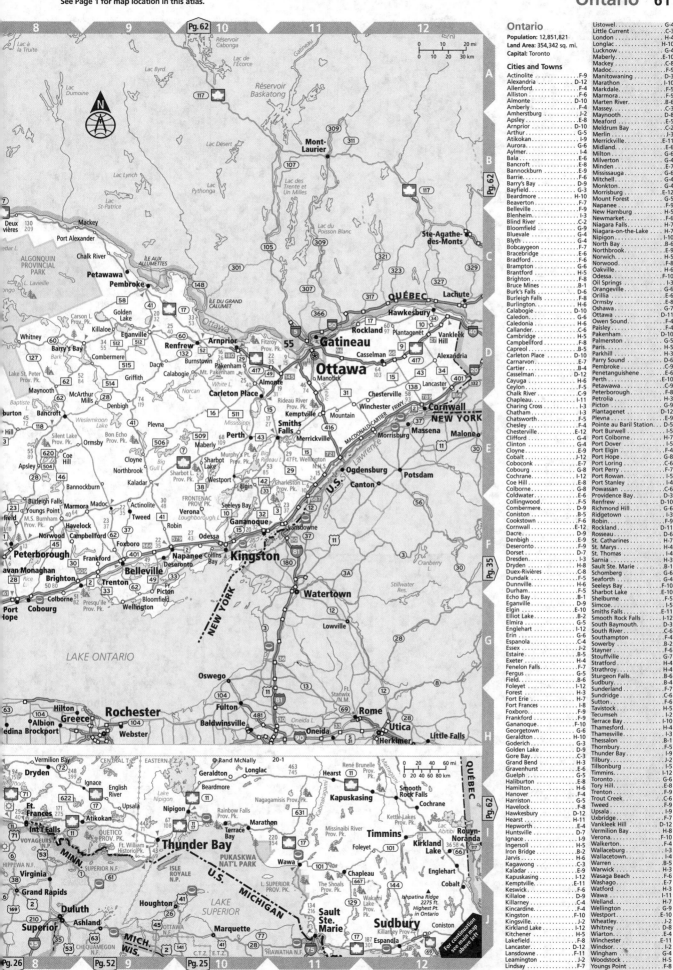

Ontario

Population: 12,851,821
Land Area: 354,342 sq. mi.
Capital: Toronto

Cities and Towns

Québec
Population: 7,903,001
Land Area: 527,079 sq. mi.
Capital: Québec

Cities and Towns

For continuation see inset below

Pg. 63 Pg. 24 Pg. 55 Pg. 61

For continuation see main map below

For continuation see inset main map above

NOTE: Maps are not always in alphabetical order.
See Page 1 for map location in this atlas.

Atlantic Provinces 63

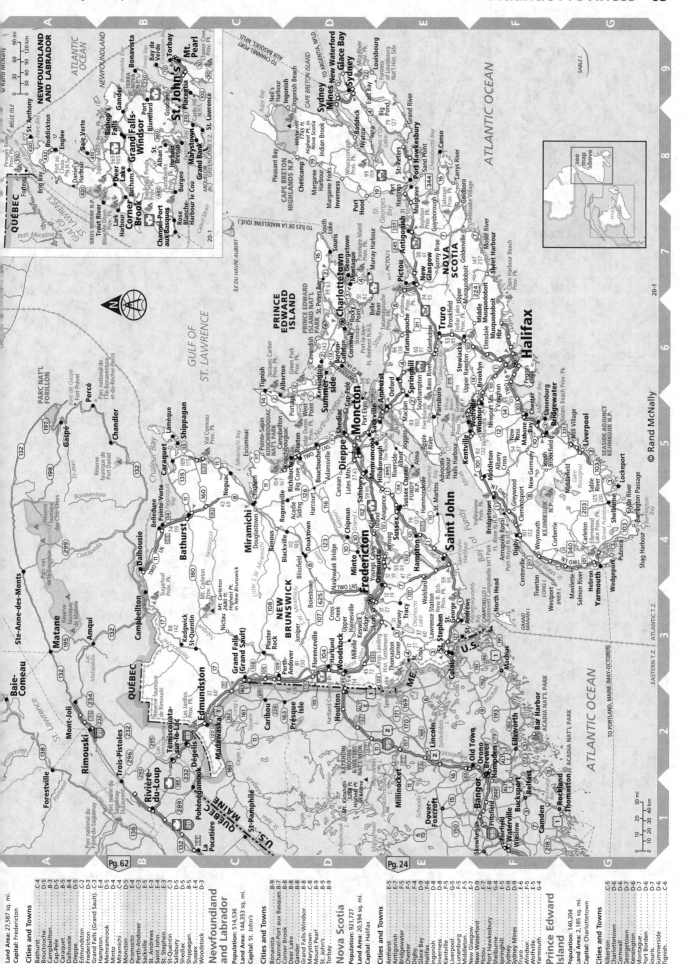

© Rand McNally

Newfoundland and Labrador

Land Area: 144,353 sq. mi.

Population: 514,536

Cities and Towns
St. John's C-8

Nova Scotia

Land Area: 20,594 sq. mi.

Population: 921,727

Cities and Towns

Amherst	E-5
Antigonish	E-7
Bridgewater	F-5
Chester	F-5
Digby	F-4
Glace Bay	D-9
Halifax	F-6
Ingonish	D-8
Kentville	E-5
Liverpool	F-5
Lunenburg	F-5
Middleton	E-5
New Glasgow	E-7
New Waterford	D-9
Port Hawkesbury	E-7
Shelburne	G-4
Springhill	E-5
Sydney	D-9
Sydney Mines	D-9
Truro	E-6
Windsor	E-5
Wolfville	E-5
Yarmouth	G-4

Prince Edward Island

Land Area: 2,185 sq. mi.

Population: 140,204

Cities and Towns

Alberton	C-5
Charlottetown	D-6
Cornwall	D-6
Georgetown	D-7
Kensington	D-6
Montague	D-7
Port Borden	D-6
Souris	D-7
Summerside	D-6
Tignish	C-5

Capital: St. John's

Capital: Halifax

Capital: Charlottetown

New Brunswick

Bathurst	C-4
Bouctouche	D-5
Campbellton	B-3
Cap-Pele	D-5
Caraquet	B-4
Dalhousie	B-3
Dieppe	D-5
Edmundston	C-2
Fredericton	D-3
Hampton	E-4
Memramcook	D-5
Minto	D-4
Miramichi	C-4
Moncton	D-5
Oromocto	D-4
Perth-Andover	C-3
Sackville	D-5
St. Andrews	E-3
St. Quentin	C-3
St. Stephen	E-3
Saint John	E-4
Salisbury	D-5
Shediac	D-5
Shippagan	B-4
Sussex	D-4
Tracadie-Sheila	C-4
Woodstock	D-3

Land Area: 27,587 sq. mi.

Capital: Fredericton

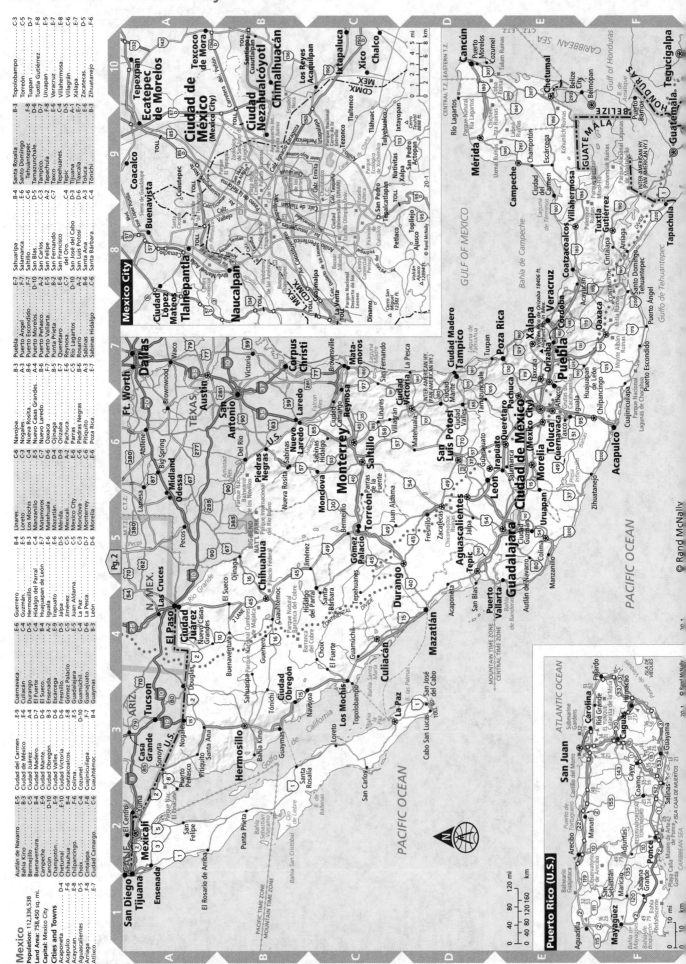

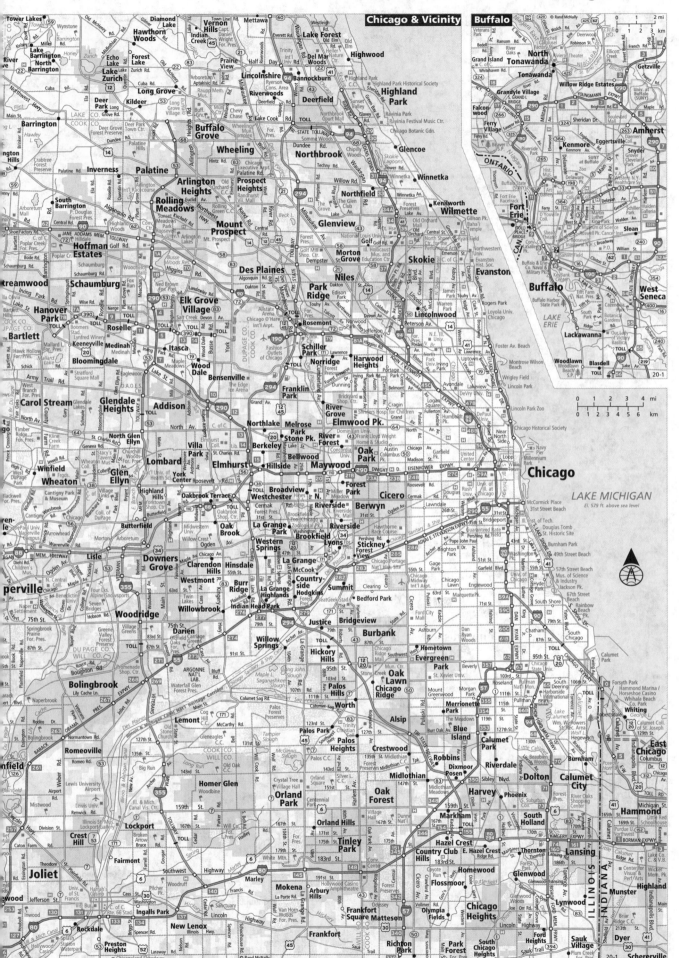

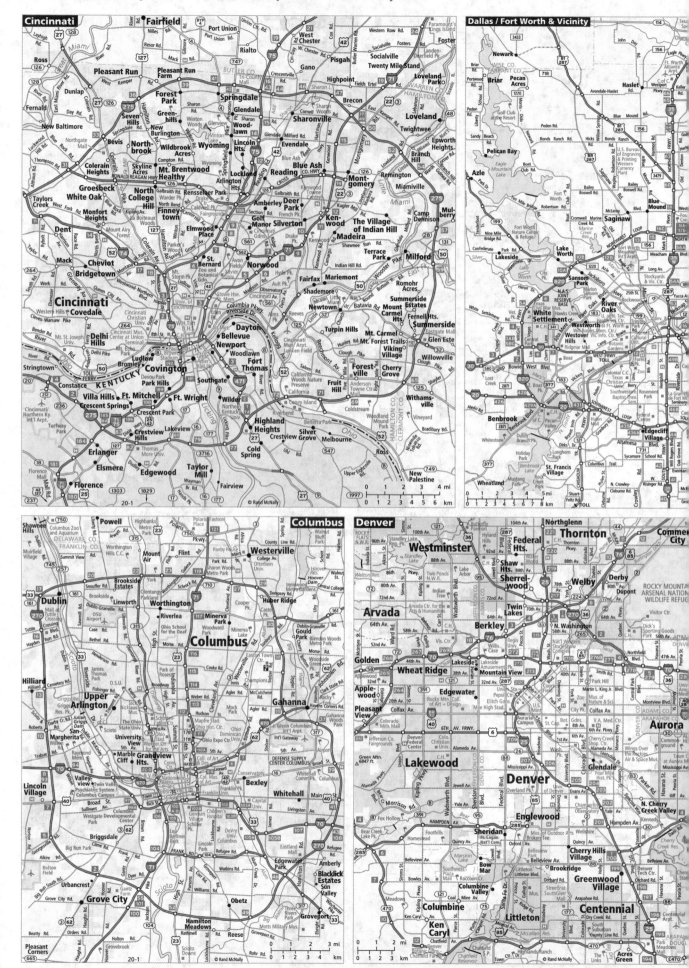

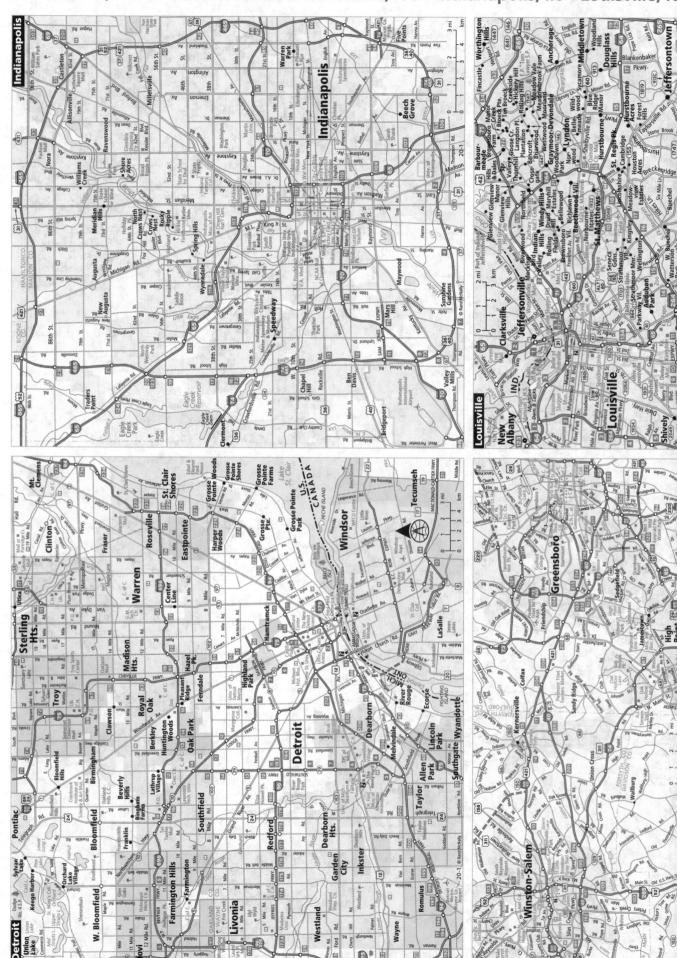

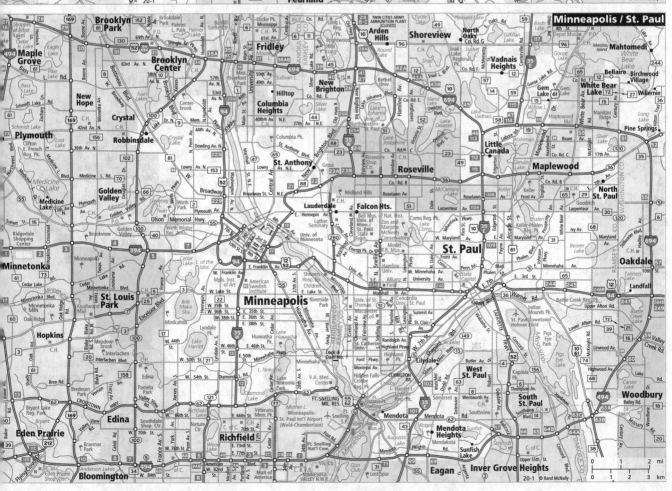

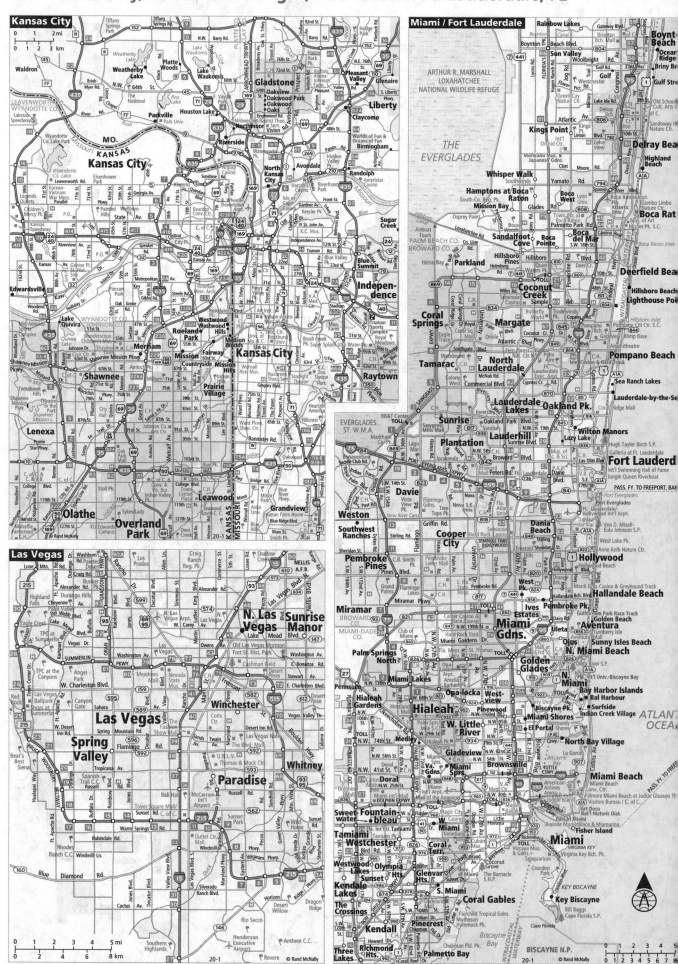

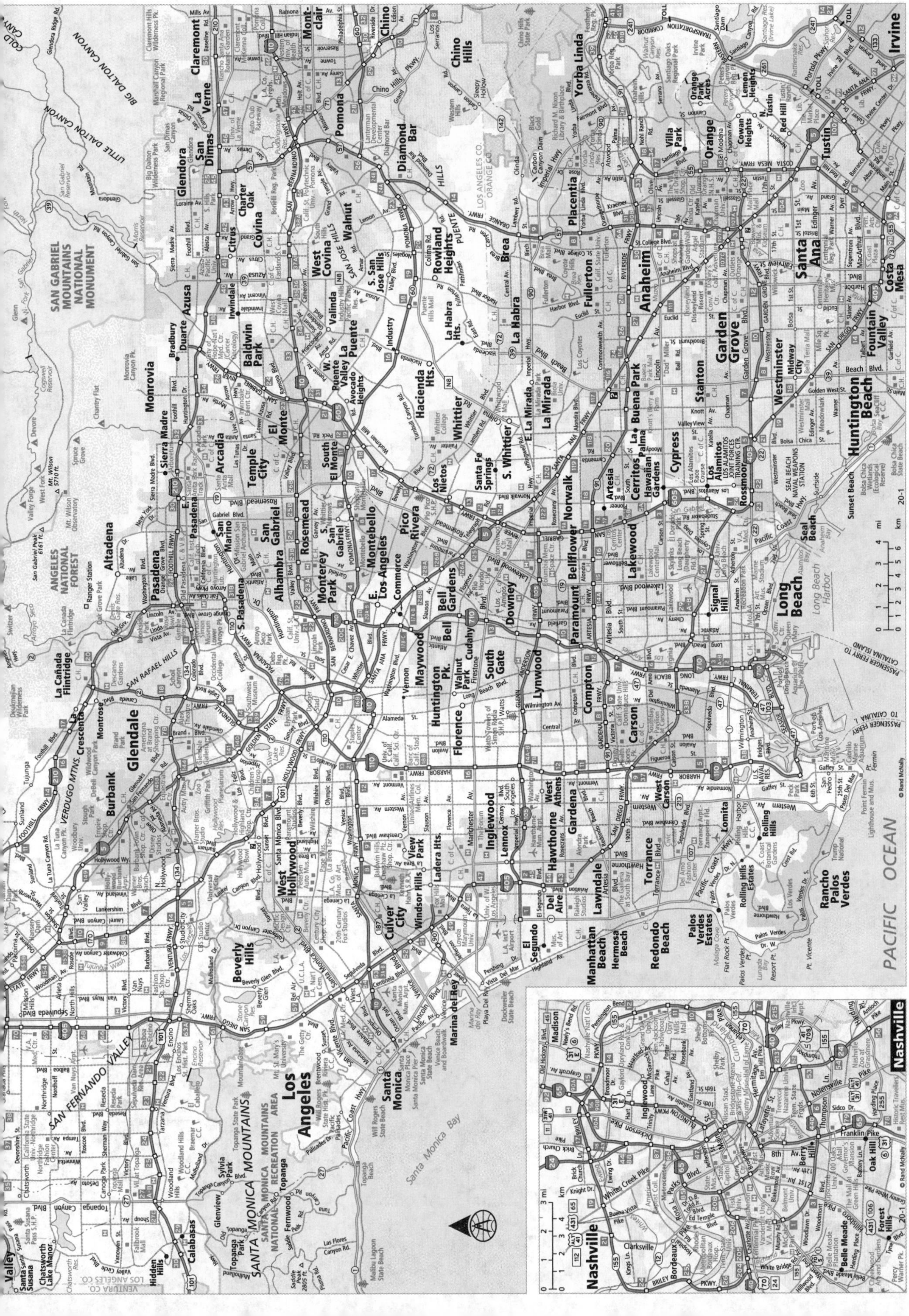

PACIFIC OCEAN
Santa Monica Bay
Los Angeles
Nashville
SAN GABRIEL MOUNTAINS NATIONAL MONUMENT
ANGELES NATIONAL FOREST
SANTA MONICA MOUNTAINS NATIONAL RECREATION AREA
SAN FERNANDO VALLEY
Santa Monica
Beverly Hills
West Hollywood
Glendale
Burbank
Pasadena
Long Beach
Anaheim
Santa Ana
Irvine
Torrance
Inglewood
Pomona
Fullerton
Huntington Beach
Garden Grove
Costa Mesa
Downey
Whittier
Compton
Carson
Norwalk
© Rand McNally

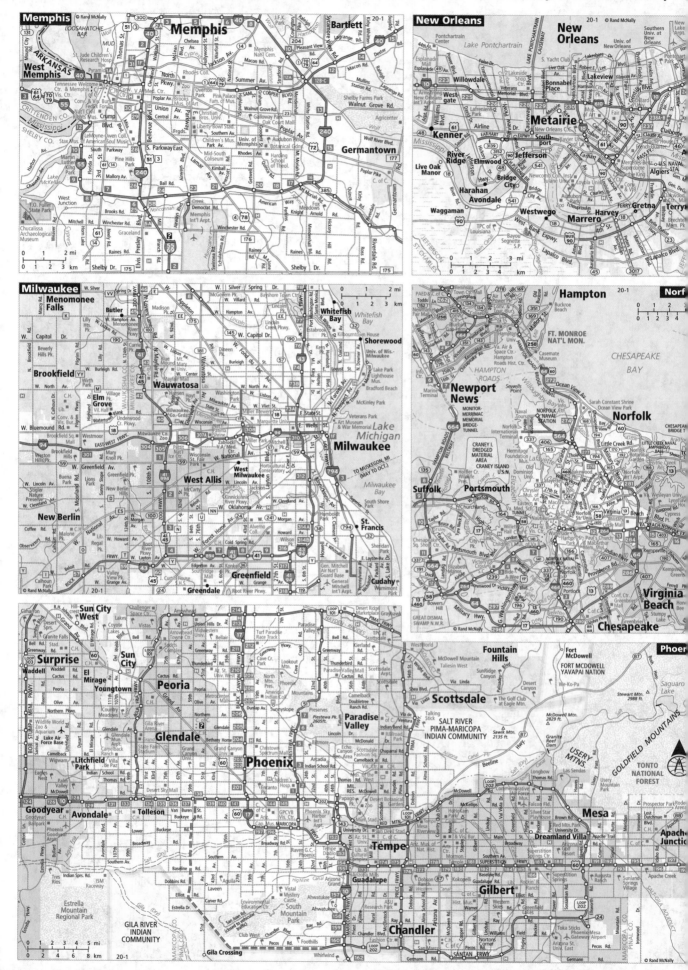

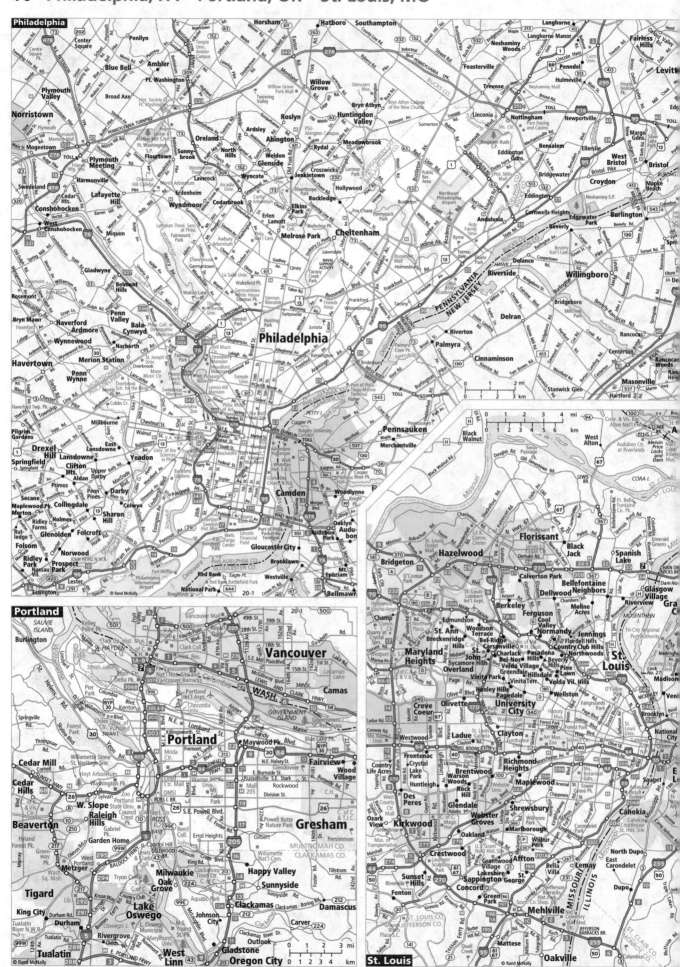

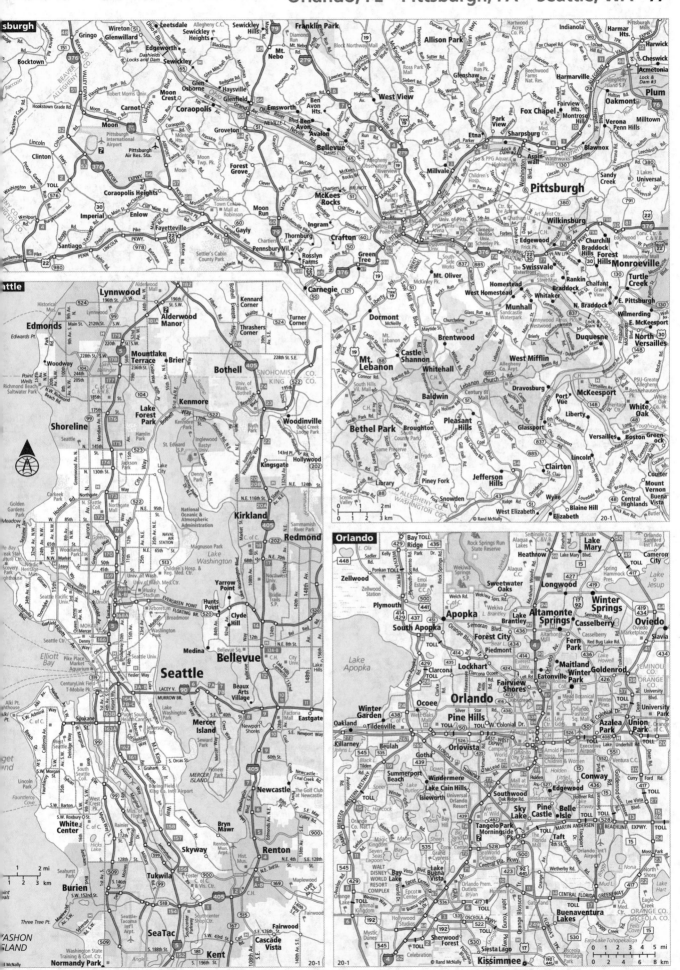

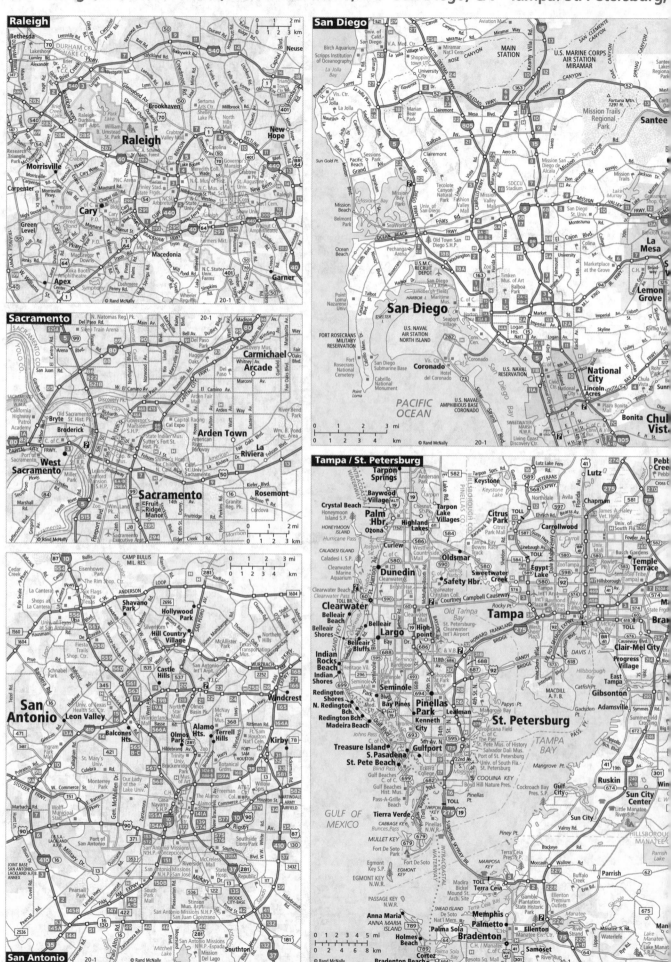

San Francisco Bay Area:
San Francisco /
Oakland / San Jose

Hotel Resources

est Western Hotels & Resorts
00) 780-7234
ww.bestwestern.com

udget Host
00) 283-4678
ww.budgethost.com

hoice Hotels
77) 424-6423

larion Hotels
ww.choicehotels.com/clarion

omfort Inn & Comfort Suites
ww.choicehotels.com/
omfort-inn
ww.choicehotels.com/
omfort-suites

conoLodge
ww.choicehotels.com/
cono-lodge

lainStay Suites
ww.choicehotels.com/mainstay

uality Inn Hotels
ww.choicehotels.com/
uality-inn

odeway Inn
ww.choicehotels.com/
odeway-inn

leep Inn
ww.choicehotels.com/sleep-inn

oast Hotels & Resorts
00) 716-6199
ww.coasthotels.com

rury Hotels
00) 378-7946
ww.druryhotels.com

xtended Stay America
00) 804-3724
ww.extendedstayamerica.com

airmont
00) 257-7544
ww.fairmont.com

our Seasons
00) 819-5053
ww.fourseasons.com

Hilton
(800) 445-8667

Doubletree
www.doubletree3.hilton.com

Embassy Suites
www.embassysuites3.hilton.com

Hampton Inn
(877) 214-6722
hamptoninn3.hilton.com

Hilton Hotels
www3.hilton.com

Homewood Suites by Hilton
homewoodsuites3.hilton.com

Hyatt Hotels & Resorts
(800) 233-1234
www.hyatt.com

Intercontinental Hotels Group
(800) 439-4745

Candlewood Suites
(888) 226-3539
www.ihg.com/candlewood

Crowne Plaza Hotel & Resorts
(877) 227-6963
www.crowneplaza.com

Holiday Inn & Holiday Inn Express
(800) 465-4329
www.holidayinn.com

Hotel Indigo
(866) 246-3446
www.hotelindigo.com

InterContinental Hotels & Resorts
(888) 424-6835
(800) 424-6835
www.intercontinental.com

Kimpton Hotels
(800) 546-7866
www.kimptonhotels.com
www.ihg.com/kimptonhotels

Staybridge Suites
(800) 238-8000
www.staybridge.com

La Quinta Hotels/Inns & Suites
(800) 753-3757
www.lq.com

Loews Hotels
(844) 241-3428
www.loewshotels.com

Marriott
Aloft Hotels
(877) 462-5638
aloft-hotels.marriott.com

Courtyard by Marriott
(800) 321-2211
courtyard.marriott.com

Delta Hotels & Resorts
(888) 890-3222
deltahotels.marriott.com

Fairfield Inn & Suites
(800) 228-2800
fairfield.marriott.com

Four Points by Sheraton
(800) 368-7764
four-points.marriott.com

Le Méridien Hotels & Resorts
(800) 543-4300
le-meridien.marriott.com

Marriott & JW Marriott
(800) 228-9290
www.marriott.com
www.marriott.com/jw-marriott

Renaissance Hotels
(800) 468-3571
renaissance-hotels.marriott.com

Residence Inn
(800) 331-3131
www.residenceinn.marriott.com

The Ritz-Carlton
(800) 542-8680
(800) 241-3333
www.ritzcarlton.com

Sheraton Hotels & Resorts
(800) 325-3535
sheraton.marriott.com

St. Regis
(877) 787-3447
st-regis.marriott.com

W Hotels
(877) 946-8357
w-hotels.marriott.com

Westin Hotels & Resorts
(800) 937-8461
westin.marriott.com

Motel 6
(800) 899-9841
www.motel6.com

Omni Hotels & Resorts
(888) 444-6664
www.omnihotels.com

Preferred Hotels & Resorts
(866) 990-9491
preferredhotels.com

Radisson
Park Inn by Radisson
(800) 670-7275
www.parkinn.com

Radisson Hotels & Resorts
(800) 967-9033
www.radisson.com

Red Lion
America's Best Inns & Suites
(855) 537-4573
www.redlion.com/americas-best-inns-suites

America's Best Value Inn
(888) 315-2378
www.redlion.com/americas-best-value-inns-suites

Jameson Inns
(855) 527-4138
www.redlion.com/jameson-inn

Knights Inn
(800) 646-5383
www.knightsinn.com

Red Lion Hotels/Red Lion Inns & Suites
(844) 248-7467
www.redlion.com

Red Roof Inn
(800) 733-7663
www.redroof.com

Wyndham
AmericInn
(800) 634-3444
www.wyndhamhotels.com/americinn

Baymont Inn & Suites
(800) 337-0550
www.wyndhamhotels.com/baymont

Days Inn
(800) 225-3297
www.wyndhamhotels.com/days-inn

Howard Johnson
(800) 221-5801
www.wyndhamhotels.com/hojo

Microtel Inns & Suites
(800) 337-0050
www.wyndhamhotels.com/microtel

Ramada Worldwide
(800) 854-9517
www.wyndhamhotels.com/ramada

Super 8
(800) 454-3213
www.wyndhamhotels.com/super-8

Travelodge
(800) 525-4055
www.wyndhamhotels.com/travelodge

Wyndham Hotels & Resorts
(877) 999-3223
www.wyndhamhotels.com/wyndham

NOTE: All toll-free reservation numbers are for the U.S. and Canada unless otherwise noted. These numbers were accurate at press time but are subject to change.

Mileage Chart

This handy chart offers more than 2,400 mileages covering 77 North American cities. Want more mileages? Visit randmcnally.com/MC and type in any two cities or addresses.

From	Albuquerque, NM	Atlanta, GA	Billings, MT	Boston, MA	Charlotte, NC	Chicago, IL	Cincinnati, OH	Dallas, TX	Denver, CO	Detroit, MI	Houston, TX	Indianapolis, IN	Kansas City, MO	Los Angeles, CA	Memphis, TN	Miami, FL	Milwaukee, WI	Minneapolis, MN	New Orleans, LA	New York, NY	Omaha, NE	Orlando, FL	Philadelphia, PA	Phoenix, AZ	Pittsburgh, PA	Portland, OR	St. Louis, MO	Salt Lake City, UT	San Francisco, CA	Seattle, WA	Washington, DC	Wichita, KS
Albuquerque, NM		1386	998	2219	1626	1333	1387	647	446	1570	884	1279	784	786	1008	1952	1354	1225	1165	2001	863	1730	1924	425	1641	1363	1037	599	1086	1438	1885	591
Amarillo, TX	288	1102	965	1935	1342	1049	1103	363	424	1286	589	995	570	1072	720	1668	1132	1009	881	1716	647	1446	1640	746	1357	1669	752	883	1370	1743	1600	418
Atlanta, GA	1386		1831	1095	244	715	461	780	1404	722	794	533	800	2174	379	661	809	1127	468	882	992	440	780	1844	684	2603	555	1878	2472	2649	637	955
Atlantic City, NJ	1985	831	2072	338	590	818	632	1518	1792	644	1598	703	1187	2774	1063	1248	910	1232	1273	126	1272	1038	60	2447	365	2922	948	2201	2934	2889	188	1379
Austin, TX	705	920	1495	1959	1164	1121	1128	196	950	1358	163	1067	702	1381	643	1341	1204	1136	503	1737	839	1124	1658	1010	1411	2068	825	1304	1760	2143	1524	542
Baltimore, MD	1887	683	1953	400	442	699	513	1368	1673	524	1448	584	1068	2670	914	1082	792	1112	1124	192	1153	889	97	2349	246	2804	829	2081	2816	2771	39	1260
Billings, MT	998	1831		2236	1990	1246	1546	1425	551	1535	1652	1435	1026	1240	1477	2497	1173	838	1868	2041	845	2275	2011	1210	1713	891	1278	552	1173	818	1951	1064
Birmingham, AL	1241	146	1780	1177	390	660	466	636	1329	724	668	478	749	2030	233	746	754	1072	343	960	939	534	880	1700	748	2551	502	1826	2327	2598	745	810
Boise, ID	938	2177	621	2660	2336	1693	1702	830	1969	1930	1835	1872	842	1825	2844	3182	1461	2216	2465	1225	2262	2435	914	2177	431	1622	340	639	503	2375	1338	
Boston, MA	2219	1095	2236		841	983	870	1764	1970	724	1844	937	1421	2983	1312	1482	1074	1396	1520	216	1436	1288	306	2681	570	3086	1182	2365	3098	3054	439	1613
Branson, MO	864	652	1241	1433	868	545	601	435	806	784	602	493	209	1651	274	1284	630	643	597	1201	402	1062	1138	1326	851	2013	249	1288	1950	2060	1081	292
Calgary, AB	1542	2357	541	2615	2400	1627	1925	1967	1096	1916	2209	1814	1567	1557	2028	3018	1555	1221	2419	2439	1387	2797	2391	1524	2093	787	1820	869	1500	678	2334	1606
Charleston, SC	1703	319	2133	970	209	908	620	1099	1706	826	1105	726	1103	2491	696	583	1002	1324	742	768	1294	380	668	2165	654	2904	857	2180	2789	2951	532	1272
Charlotte, NC	1626	244	1990	841		769	477	1023	1566	616	1038	583	961	2414	619	728	867	1180	712	641	1151	526	539	2088	446	2761	714	2037	2712	2808	398	1092
Chicago, IL	1333	715	1246	983	769		289	926	1002	282	1085	181	526	2015	531	1381	90	408	923	787	470	1153	757	1795	459	2118	295	1398	2130	2063	697	724
Cincinnati, OH	1387	461	1546	870	477	289		934	1187	259	1055	109	584	2172	482	1127	381	703	804	637	722	905	571	1849	288	2369	348	1647	2380	2363	512	779
Cleveland, OH	1598	714	1597	638	514	344	248	1194	1330	169	1315	315	799	2342	729	1240	434	756	1057	460	797	1043	428	2060	134	2446	534	1725	2458	2414	370	992
Columbus, OH	1457	567	1606	763	426	354	107	1039	1261	212	1174	189	657	2244	587	1164	445	766	910	533	792	954	468	1920	174	2439	421	1718	2451	2425	411	851
Corpus Christi, TX	855	1001	1622	2051	1244	1338	1262	410	1077	1542	207	1228	919	1494	782	1394	1421	1353	554	1844	1056	1172	1754	1122	1561	2218	1042	1454	1873	2292	1619	758
Dallas, TX	647	780	1425	1764	1023	926	934		880	1163	239	873	489	1437	453	1307	1010	928	519	1548	656	1086	1467	1066	1221	2128	630	1403	1734	2193	1332	361
Denver, CO	446	1404	551	1970	1566	1002	1187	880		1270	1035	1083	603	1015	1097	2069	1042	913	1398	1775	534	1851	1732	908	1447	1256	854	533	1268	1320	1671	519
Des Moines, IA	983	902	946	1299	1057	335	580	683	670	599	938	474	194	1682	617	1567	375	244	1008	1105	135	1339	1074	1445	777	1786	350	1065	1798	1764	1015	391
Detroit, MI	1570	722	1535	724	616	282	259	1163	1270			277	764	2281	742	1354	374	696	1066	613	736	1144	583	2032	285	2345	533	1664	2937	2513	522	964
Duluth, MN	1375	1187	860	1370	1239	466	760	1092	1063	754	1331	651	586	2076	963	1852	394	152	1354	1264	530	1632	1230	1838	932	1749	679	1458	2033	1677	1171	785
Edmonton, AB	1724	2391	722	2549	2443	1670	1968	2149	1278	1958	2391	1857	1626	1755	2147	3058	1598	1264	2538	2482	1445	2836	2434	1721	2136	966	1878	1069	1695	793	2377	1787
El Paso, TX	266	1418	1257	2373	1662	1455	1569	635	707	1702	744	1398	929	796	1089	1934	1497	1377	1095	2202	1004	1712	2102	424	1774	1630	1157	866	1175	1705	1967	730
Fargo, ND	1318	1361	607	1629	1414	641	937	1079	873	930	1321	825	600	1848	1054	2025	569	234	1445	1438	427	1805	1405	1780	1707	1191	841	1150	1793	1424	1348	685
Gatlinburg, TN	1439	196	1803	922	202	578	290	884	1376	552	964	396	773	2226	431	865	672	994	640	707	964	640	625	1901	493	2574	527	1850	2525	2621	490	905
Guadalajara, JA	1194	1739	2194	2789	1982	1954	1962	1028	1639	2191	948	1901	1535	1501	1482	2131	2037	1969	1292	2592	1672	1910	2492	1212	2261	2545	1658	1792	1963	2631	2356	1377
Gulfport, MS	1221	399	1912	1482	643	896	767	562	1386	1025	403	780	883	1949	365	792	988	1196	78	1266	1073	572	1180	1577	1052	2633	647	1909	2307	2730	1036	867
Houston, TX	884	794	1652	1844	1038	1085	1055	239	1035	1319		1021	732	1550	575	1186	1163	1171	348	1632	898	965	1547	1178	1354	2356	784	1634	1929	2431	1411	595
Indianapolis, IN	1279	533	1435	937	583	181	109	873	1083	277	1021		482	2068	464	1198	272	591	818	707	643			1742	293	2243	243	1541		2273	582	674
Jacksonville, FL	1636	346	2183	1146	379	1068	796	992	1756	1002	871	874	1152	2421	677	349	1163	1474	547	939	1344	141	844	2050	825	2954	907	2230	2723	3001	706	1272
Kansas City, MO	784	800	1026	1421	961	526	584	489	603	764	732	482		1616	451	1466	565	436	844	1196	184	1246	1127	1246	840	1797	248	1073	1808	1844	1066	198
Key West, FL	2099	809	2646	1659	886	1534	1275	1455	2222	1515	1334	1348	1617	2884	1159	160	1632	1944	1010	1446	1807	387	1357	2514	1332	3417	1370	2693	3186	3464	1213	1735
Las Vegas, NV	572	1959	973	2714	2199	1746	1932	1220	747	2013	1457	1828	1349	270	1581	2525	1786	1656	1739	2518	1278	2303	2480	285	2190	1023	1600	419	569	1128	2428	1164
Lexington, KY	1371	369	1610	917	400	370	83	876	1186	344	996	184	581	2128	423	1030	464	782	745	701	771	817	638	1833	370	2381	334	1657	2342	2428	533	773
Little Rock, AR	877	515	1407	1447	754	650	617	319	965	885	439	583	381	1666	136	1147	724	815	425	1230	574	925	1150	1340	905	2211	345	1488	1963	2275	1015	446
Los Angeles, CA	786	2174	1240	2983	2414	2015	2172	1437	1015	2281	1550	2068	1616		1794	2735	2055	1925	1894	2787	1546	2515	2713	370	2428	963	1821	688	380	1134	2670	1377
Memphis, TN	1008	379	1477	1312	619	531	482	453	1097	742	575	464	451	1794		1012	622	831	394	1094	641	778	1014	1471	768	2245	283	1524	2095	2299	879	577
Mexico City, DF	1404	1718	2301	2768	1962	2017	1979	1090	1756	2194	963	1598	1839	1500	2111	2100	2032	1272	2571	1735	1889	2471	1469	2279	2768	1721	2003	2218	2842	2336	1440	
Miami, FL	1952	661	2497	1482	728	1381	1127	1307	2069	1354	1186	1198	1466	2735	1012		1475	1791	861	1288	1658	215	1180	2362	1173	3260	1221	2544	3038	3315	1044	1587
Milwaukee, WI	1354	809	1173	1074	867	90	381	1010	1042	374	1163	272	565	2055	622	1475		337	1015	879	509	1258	849	1817	551	2062	379	1437	2170	1990	788	763
Minneapolis, MN	1225	1127	838	1396	1180	408	703	928	913	696	1171	591	436	1925	831	1791	337		1223	1204	372	1573	1171	1687	874	1727	563	1308	2040	1655	1110	634
Mobile, AL	1234	328	1874	1427	571	917	721	589	1414	978	468	733	850	2014	382	719	1011	1224	144	1202	1038	497	1101	1643	1000	2661	645	1936	2320	2727	965	894
Montréal, QC	2129	1218	2099	310	980	847	824	1722	1832	560	1884	847	1330	2845	1314	1647	938	1262	1640	382	1302	1437	454	2591	603	2948	1092	2228	2916	2587	529	1529
Nashville, TN	1219	248	1586	1099	408	469	273	664	1158	534	786	287	555	2006	209	913	564	881	532	884	747	692	802	1682	560	2357	307	1633	2306	2404	667	688
New Orleans, LA	1165	468	1868	1520	712	923	804	519	1398	1066	348	818	844	1894	394	861	1015	1223		1304	1032	641	1222	1523	1090	2642	675	1920	2252	2716	1087	880
New York, NY	2001	882	2041	216	641	787	637	1548	1775	613	1632	707	1196	2787	1094	1288	879	1204	1304		1245	1089	95	2463	369	2891	954	2170	2902	2858	228	1391
Norfolk, VA	1910	558	2132	569	328	878	605	1350	1758	704	1362	720	1155	2707	898	950	969	1295	1026	370	1335	755	271	2373	425	2962	911	2238	2973	2949	193	1347
Oklahoma City, OK	542	844	1203	1678	1084	792	846	206	631	1029	437	739	348	1326	466	1476	876	788	722	1460	452	1254	1384	1005	1101	1922	496	1200	1627	1948	1344	160
Omaha, NE	863	992	845	1436	1151	470	722	656	534	736	898	613	184	1546	641	1658	509	372	1032	1245		1436	1212	1325	914	1650	439	930	1662	1663	1151	298
Orlando, FL	1730	440	2275	1288	526	1153	905	1086	1851	1144	965	968	1246	2515	778	235	1258	1573	641	1089	1436		986	2145	975	3048	999	2323	2816	3093	849	1365
Ottawa, ON	2039	1158	1768	428	920	760	732	1632	1748	471	1804	757	1240	2763	1230	1618	859	1032	1582	440	1213	1408	447	2501	546	2660	1002	2142	2877	2586	566	1439
Philadelphia, PA	1924	780	2011	306	539	757	511	1467	1732	560	1884	643	1127	2713	1063	1347	849	1171	1222	95	1212	986		2387	306	2861	888	2140	2873	2828	137	1319
Phoenix, AZ	425	1844	1210	2681	2088	1795	1849	1066	908	2032	1178	1742	1246	373	1471	2362	1817	1687	1523	2463	1325	2145	2387		2104	1332	1499	653	749	1414	2348	1053
Pittsburgh, PA	1641	684	1713	570	446	459	288	1221	1447	285	1354	359	840	2428	768	1173	551	874	1090	369	914	975	305	2104		2563	604	1842	2574	2530	243	1035
Portland, ME	2315	1192	2333	107	938	1079	967	1861	2067	825	1940	1034	1518	3082	1408	1585	1176	1492	1616	304	1533	1385	402	2778	666	3186	1279	2461	3196	3151	535	1710
Portland, OR	1363	2603	891	3086	2761	2118	2369	2128	1256	2385	2356	2260	1797	963	2245	3260	2062	1727	2642	2891	1650	3048	2861	1332	2563		2050	765	635	174	2800	1692
Rapid City, SD	843	1508	323	1900	1670	912	1208	1061	397	1200	1291	1100	704	1312	1160	2173	840	571	1551	1708	525	1936	1675	1305	1378	1215	959	649	1384	1142	1618	699
Reno, NV	1019	2396	958	2881	2555	1913	2163	1668	1051	2180	1904	2056	1591	470	2029	3063	1953	1818	2186	2685	1445	2841	2656	733	2357	578	1384	518	218	720	2595	1558
Richmond, VA	1832	532	2051	547	293	797	512	1278	1671	622	1329	627	1069	2620	824	944	888	1210	1002	334	1259	742	245	2294	344	2869	822	2145	2880	2868	108	1261
St. Louis, MO	1037	555	1278	1182	714	295	348	630	854	533	784	243	248	1821	284	1221	379	563	675	954	439	999	888	1499	604	2050		1326	2061	2096	827	442
Salt Lake City, UT	599	1878	552	2365	2037	1398	1647	1403	533	1646	1634	1541	1073	688	1524	2544	1437	1308	1920	2170	930	2323	2140	653	1842	765	1326		735	839	2079	1042
San Antonio, TX	712	986	1480	2039	1230	1202	1210	276	935	1439	195	1149	766	1377	1379	1285	1205	541	1822	920	1160	1742	985	1495	2076	906	1311	1736	2150	1607	625	
San Diego, CA	810	2138	1302	3046	2381	2080	2196	1472	1077	2346	1472	2089	1597	120	1819	2656	2118	1986	1816	2809	1613	2436	2738	355	2452	1083	1345	758	501	1256	2693	1401
San Francisco, CA	1086	2472	1173	3098	2712	2130	2380	1734	1268	2397	1929	2273	1808	382	2095	3038	2170	2040	2252	2902	1662	2816	2873	749	2574	635	2061	735		807	2812	1775
Santa Fe, NM	58	1379	943	2212	1618	1313	1379	640	391	1562	877	1272	766	846	998	1944	1316	1207	1158	1994	891	1723	1917	520	1634	1388	1029	625	1144	1463	1879	572
Sault Ste. Marie, ON	1777	1040	1273	923	947	483	577	1370	1428	347	1552	540	951	2465	1015	1400	545	1355	921	850	1175	911	2240	614	2166	740	1848	2581	2090	856	1117	
Seattle, WA	1438	2649	818	3054	2808	2063	2363	2193	1320	2353	2431	2253	1844	1134	2299	3315	1990	1655	2716	2858	1663	3093	2828	1414	2530	174	2096	839	807		2768	1828
Spokane, WA	1320	2369	541	2774	2528	1785	2084	1964	1091	2075	2192	1973	1564	1216	2018	3035	1712	1377	2409	2580	1383	2814	2550	1381	2252	352	1817	720	874	279	2490	1600
Tampa, FL	1746	451	2293	1342	578	1166	916	1102	1860	1178	980	984	1252	2525	779	280	1260	1578	651	1138	1445	85	1040	2153	1023	3064	1008	2340	2832	3111	904	1381
Toronto, ON	1800	963	1771	548	756	519	493	1393	1504	231	1551	518	1001	2517	983	1483	609	933	1306	489	974	1284	497	2262	316	2620	763	1899	2632	2588	486	1188
Tulsa, OK	645	782	1234	1576	1022	687	738	258	692	927	487	635	263	1433	402	1414	773	704	671	1350	380	1192	1282	1107	994	1938	392	1215	1731	2012	1234	175
Vancouver, BC	1575	2785	953	3188	2944	2198	2499	2338	1465	2487	2565	2389	1980	1275	2437	3451	2125	1790	2801	2993	1799	3229	2963	1550	2665	313	2232	973	947	141	2903	1973
Washington, DC	1885	637	1951	439	398	697	512	1332	1671	522	1411	582	1066	2670	879	1044	788	1110	1087	228	1151	849	137	2348	244	2800	827	2079	2812	2768		1258
Wichita, KS	591	955	1064	1613	1092	724	779	361	519	964	595	674	198	1377	577	1587	763	634	880	1391	298	1365	1319	1053	1035	1764	442	1042	1775	1828	1258	